PORTRAIT OF
SKYE AND THE OUTER HEBRIDES

ALSO BY W. DOUGLAS SIMPSON

Portrait of
SKYE AND THE
OUTER HEBRIDES

W. DOUGLAS SIMPSON

ILLUSTRATED
AND WITH MAPS

ROBERT HALE   LONDON

© W. Douglas Simpson 1967

First edition 1967
Reprinted 1968
Reprinted 1973
Reprinted 1975

Robert Hale & Company
63 Old Brompton Road
London S.W.7

ISBN 0 7091 0650 5

Printed and bound in Great Britain by
Redwood Burn Limited
Trowbridge & Esher

CONTENTS

ILLUSTRATIONS

MAPS

ACKNOWLEDGEMENTS

The above copyright photographs are reproduced by permission of the following: Eric G. Meadows (1, 3, 4, 6, 7, 8, 9, 11, 12, 13, 14, 15, 18, 19, 20, 21, 22, 23 and 24); Ministry of Public Building and Works (2, 10 bottom); J. Allan Cash (5, 16 and 17).

I

ISLANDS OF FANTASY

From the lone shieling on the misty island,
Mountains divide us, and a waste of seas;
Yet still the blood is strong, the heart is Highland,
And we, in dreams, behold the Hebrides.

So runs the first verse of a famous song. Yet there are countless
thousands others, beside those transatlantic exiles, who in their
dreams behold the Hebrides. Visitors they are, from Britain, from
the whole overseas English-speaking world, and from many other
nations besides, who come to make acquaintance with these
remarkable islands, and with their no less remarkable inhabitants.
You may return from the Hebrides loving or hating them; but
never afterwards will you be indifferent to them. The utter
strangeness, indeed often the sheer fantastic impact of their
scenery, with its combination and contrast of mountain and moorland, fiord and loch; their stupendous geology, and their natural
history so rich and diverse; the ancient and beautiful language
spoken by their inhabitants, which for years has been proclaimed
as moribund, but yet stubbornly survives; their distinctive and
old-world culture, which is usually ignored, and not seldom has
been denied—all these aspects of the Hebrides combine to make
an enduring impression upon the observant eye and upon the
mind still unsurrendered to the modern means of mass indoctrina-
tion.

The existence, on the western fringe of the Scottish Highlands,
of a scenery so wholly different from anything else in Britain; of a
language that carries us back to a time before any English was
spoken in England; of a society retaining so many primitive
characteristics amid the dull uniformity of twentieth century
materialism—all this confronts the philosophic visitor with much
food for serious thought. Nothing, within the likely span of
survival to which the human race may look forward, will greatly
alter the scenery of the Hebrides; but if in due course the Gaelic

language and the distinctive social characteristics of the Scottish
Highlander are indeed doomed to extinction—then all that can
be said is that, when that ill day dawns, Scotland will be a far less
interesting country.

The word Hebrides is a misnomer, due to a blundered tran-
script of the name Haebudes or Hebudes, applied to the Western
Isles by the Roman *savant* Pliny. Nobody knows the meaning of
the name; it has been thought to be pre-Celtic. Needless to say,
the scholars of classical antiquity had only the vaguest notion of
the Western Isles. In his biography of Julius Agricola, the famous
Roman governor of Britain, Tacitus gives us a brief though
accurate description of the western coast of Scotland:

> Nowhere has the sea a wider dominion: it has many currents
> running in every direction; it does not merely flow and ebb within
> the limits of the shore, but penetrates and winds far inland, and finds
> a home among hills and mountains as though in its own domain.

But of the Hebrid Isles, out in the open ocean beyond this
indented coastline, Tacitus tells us nothing; though, in the far
north, he was well aware of the existence of the Orkney and
Shetland Islands. We know that Agricola's fleet circumnavigated
Scotland: and it has been suggested that two scraps of first-century
Samian ware, found in the Everley broch in Caithness, could be a
relic of this expedition.

In Ptolemy's famous map, drawn in the second century, and
doubtless embodying the information gathered by Agricola's
soldiers and marines, *Scitis insula* is certainly Skye; and it is more
than likely that *Dumna*—one of the places for which Ptolemy had
bearings—is Lewis; the name is thought to signify "the deep-sea
island". Pliny knew of the existence of thirty Hebudes. A Greek
writer, Demetrius of Tarsus, informs us that off the shores of
Britain lie many small and desolate islands, inhabited only by
spirits and demigods, mild and gracious in their lives, but whose
passing was accompanied by mighty storms. The mention of
numerous and desolate islands and frequent storms implies some
dim knowledge of the Hebrides. Hardly less fantastic is the account
given of them by an anonymous Roman geographer of the later
Empire. The inhabitants of the islands know naught of agriculture,
they live on fish and milk. One king rules over them all, for although the islands are numerous they are separated only by

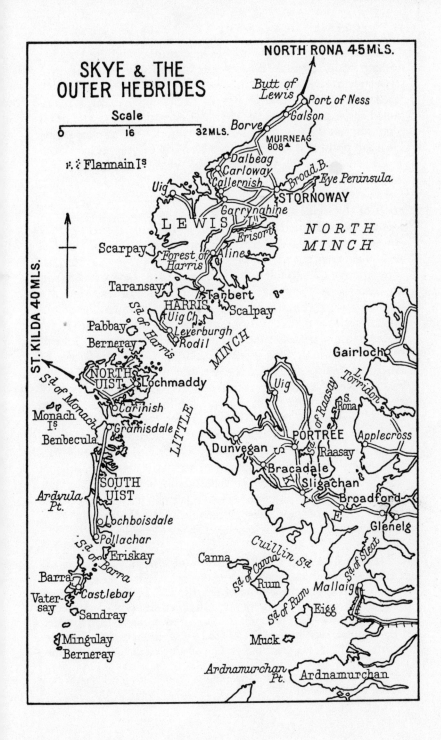

narrow straits. All things are held in common, and the king has nothing of his own. In the interests of equity he is bound by a strict code of laws. From avarice he is saved by his poverty, which teaches him justice, since he has no private income, but is maintained at the public expense. He is not even allowed a wife of his own, but has the use in turn of whatever women take his fancy. He is not permitted to beget children. All in all, it must have been a dim job being the Celtic King of the Isles! Things became better for his successors after the coming of the Norse.

Ten centuries after the fall of the Western Empire, in the high noon of the Renaissance, a distinguished scholar of international repute, the friend and correspondent of Erasmus, namely Hector Boece, first Principal of Aberdeen University, a native of Dundee, and on every count a man who ought to have known better, has some strange tales to tell us of the Hebrides. In Lewis, he informs us, there is only one river: it is plentiful in salmon,[1] but if a woman wade through it in springtime, no salmon will be caught for the rest of that year! From his narrative it appears that Hector Boece had not landed in Lewis: but he did visit some at least of the Hebrides, in company with Alexander Galloway, Rector of Aberdeen University, and, like the Principal, a man of learning and culture. Yet between them these two renowned apostles of the Scottish Renaissance are responsible for the marvellous yarn of the "claik geese" of the Hebrides. It deserves to be reproduced in the picturesque language of Boece's sixteenth-century translator, John Bellenden. After gravely assuring us that these "barnacle geese" were not generated in the worm-eaten cavities of drift wood, which he calls a "vane opinioun" among "the rude and ignorant pepil", he proceeds to relate the scientific facts as to the generation of these seafowl from mussels, as he and Galloway had observed it with their own eyes in the Hebrides:

Maister Alexander Galloway, Person of Kinkell, was with us in thir Ilis, gevand his mind, with maist ernist besines, to serche the verite of thir obscure and misty dowtis; and, be adventure, liftet up ane see-tangle, hingand full of mussill schellis fra the rute to the branchis. Sone efter, he opnit ane of thir mussill schellis: bot than he was mair astonist than afore; for he saw na fische in it, bot ane perfit schapin foule, smal and gret ay effering to the quantite of the

[1] About twenty years later, Dean Monro, writing in 1549, knew of eight salmon rivers in Lewis.

schell. This Clerk, knawin us richt desirus of sic uncouth thingis, come haistely with the said tangle, and opnit it to us, with all circumstance afore rehersit.

The geese-bearing mussels, he tells us, bore their way into rotten driftwood, and in these cavities the barnacle geese are generated:

first, thay schaw thair heid and feit, and last of all thay schaw thair plumis and wingis; finaly, quhen thay ar cumin to the just mesure and quantite of geis, thay fle in the aire as othir fowlis dois.

When, from the ninth century onwards, the Norsemen extended their control, first over the Shetlands and Orkneys and then over the Hebrides, they styled the former group the *Nordereys* or Northern Isles, and the latter the *Sudereys*, the Southern Isles. In due course Norwegian control was extended as far south as Man, and so the Norse diocese of the Western Isles came to be known as the Bishopric of Sodor and Man. In the mid-twelfth century the Norse realm of the Sudereys, which we may style the Kingdom of Man and the Isles, was disrupted by the successful career of Somerled, *regulus* or sub-king of Ergadia—that is to say Argyll, a region which then extended along the western coast from the Mull of Kintyre as far north as Loch Broom. Gaining a great sea victory over the King of Man and the Isles in 1156, Somerled forced upon him a division of the Hebrides, taking into his own power the islands south of the Point of Ardnamurchan. Thus were formed two separate realms—both still under the waning overlordship of the King of Norway. This division into Northern and Southern Hebrides has often been confused with the Norse terms already explained, namely the *Nordereys*, i.e. the Shetlands and Orkneys, and *Sudereys*, i.e. the Hebrides as a whole. Somerled's partition of the Sudereys left a permanent mark upon Hebridean history, which was not extinguished by their gradual absorption into the Scottish realm after Alexander III's victory over Haakon IV at Largs in 1263, and the Treaty of Perth three years later, whereby the Sudereys were ceded to Scotland. Indeed it is probable that the partition made by Somerled did no more than underline a cleavage dating back to times far more remote. As a modern scholar has written:[1]

[1] Sir Warren Lindsay Scott, "The Norse in the Hebrides", in *The Viking Congress, Lerwick, July 1950*, p. 193.

The Southern Hebrides—the islands south of Ardnamurchan—had been colonised from Ireland by the Dalriadic Scots, and the great sanctuary of Iona had been established in 565. St Columba's life, written by his distinguished successor St Adamnan about 690, gives us a distinct, if limited, picture of these southern islands, but it strongly suggests that north of Ardnamurchan there was an alien world which the saint could not penetrate, and of which Adamnan himself had but slight knowledge. Only once[1] did Columba enter these non-Scotic lands, when he visited for a few days the coast of Skye and baptised a chief called by the Celtic name of Artbrannan, to whom, however, he spoke only through an interpreter.

It is with the Northern Hebrides, as thus defined by Somerled's partition, that we are concerned in this book. They divide themselves into two groups, an inner and an outer. The former comprises Skye and the Small Isles—Canna, Rum, Eigg and Muck, all of which are in Inverness-shire. The outer group, collectively known as the Long Island, consist of Lewis with Harris, North Uist, Benbecula, South Uist, Eriskay and Barra, besides various smaller islets not needful to be listed here. Lewis belongs to the shire of Ross and Cromarty; the remainder of the Long Island is part of Inverness-shire.

The Inner and Outer Isles are sundered by the wide stormy channel known as the Minch. But the division between the two groups is far more than a mere matter of geography. The older geologists used to define them respectively as the Trap Islands and the Gneiss Islands. Although the word "trap" is now no longer current among the fraternity of the hammer, its convenient compactness may serve to underline the fact that the Inner Hebrides, north of Ardnamurchan, represent, broadly speaking, the dissected fragments of a vast volcanic pile built up in Eocene times. Of this stupendous igneous episode an account in some detail will be given when we come to look at Skye. By contrast, the Long Island consists almost wholly of metamorphic rocks, gneisses and schists which have undergone fundamental changes through vast tectonic stresses and prolonged pneumatolysis—that is to say, chemical alteration brought about under high temperatures and enormous pressures. All these complex intervolved

---

[1] But it is well to remember that this is the only occasion that happens to be recorded by Adamnan. Any *argumentum ex silentio* based on his tantalising book is highly dangerous.

processes, it must be understood, were in train throughout an incalculable lapse of time, and were completed unsummed aeons before the first lowly forms of life appeared upon our globe. It is not surprising that among these "Lewisian Gneisses" geologists have recognized some of the oldest rocks so far identified in the earth's crust.

After these stupendous processes had been accomplished, the pile of hard crystalline rocks thus formed was elevated to form a land surface. In the course of ages this plateau was dissected by weathering into a complex of mountains and valleys. Once more the land sank into a broad *cuvette* or basin of deposition; and here, in shallow fresh water and under torrential conditions, was laid down a very famous deposit, the Torridonian Sandstone, a dark brown or purplish formation which occupies part of the Sleat peninsula in Skye, the northern half of Rum, and (perhaps) an area round Broad Bay, north of Stornoway in Lewis. (See *infra*. p. 117). Despite their age, the Torridonians are almost unaltered; and the shallow-water conditions under which they accumulated are clearly visible today in the presence of ripple marks, sun cracks, and raindrop pittings such as you may see on any modern sand beach. Worm-tracks and other obscure organic traces reveal that life in its lowliest forms has already emerged upon our globe.

The later geological chronicle of the Northern Hebrides will be resumed in detail when we come to look at Skye. Meantime enough has been said to justify the claim of Sir Archibald Geikie, that the fossil landscape of mountain and glen, carved out of Lewisian Gneiss and now sealed by the Torridonian Sandstone, is "the oldest known fragment of Europe".[1] The visitor who lands on Lewis sets foot upon the very foundation stones of Britain. And if a visitor to Skye take his stand on a clear day upon the eastern cliffs of Trotternish, in the neighbourhood of Staffin, and looks across the Inner Sound north-eastward to the mainland, he will mark the striking contrast between the low rounded platform of grey Lewisian gneiss and the huge isolated domes of dark red Torridonian sandstone that rest upon it.

We shall find that the nameless races who have successively settled in the Northern Hebrides at least since Mesolithic times have left abundant traces of their presence in the numerous cairns, *duns*, brochs, earth-houses, and portable antiquities which have been recorded from all the isles. By the dawn of the Christian

---

[1] *Scenery of Scotland*, 3rd ed. (1901), p. 125.

era the population contained a strong Celtic element, as the place names show; and the missionaries of the Celtic Church, from Ireland and elsewhere, have left enduring memories in the remains or sites of their monasteries and chapels, the holy wells and sculptured stones that mark their wanderings, and the dim legends that have gathered round their mighty shades.

That the Norse colonists were no more than a dominant minority, that they did not extirpate the native populations, but in due course blent with them to form the mixed breed known in our chronicles as the *Gallgael*, "foreign Gaels", is sufficiently shown by the fact that, whereas in the Nordereys the language and the place names became almost wholly Norse, in the Sudereys the Gaelic speech remains to this day; while the place names, Norse as against Celtic, vary from an estimated 80 per cent in Lewis to 66 per cent in North Uist and in Skye; 33 per cent or thereabouts, in Islay; 20 per cent on the peninsula of Kintyre; and 11 per cent in Arran. In the Hebrides generally, Norse graves are conspicuous by their rarity; and it is significant that they are the graves of warrior chiefs, not of peasant colonists as in Orkney and Shetland.

In the Outer Hebrides, there appears to be some evidence that, when the Norse landings began, the native population was in a state of slow decline, due to two causes: the growth of blanket peat in the interiors, and the drowning of the fertile *machair*-land on the western shores through land submergence.[1] Upon the whole, it seems likely that, by the time of Somerled's partition, the Northern Hebrides had fallen behind the Southern in development, partly owing to the more intensive Norse raiding and settlement and partly because the southern group were more closely in touch with the superior civilization of Ireland. This could have been one of the reasons why Somerled chose the southern group for himself.

By the closing years of the ninth century such famous warriors as Ketil Flatnose had made their homes in the Northern Hebrides, and had been more or less converted to Christianity—though it is recorded of one of them, Helgi the Lean, a Hebridean born, that "he prayed to Christ at home but to Thor in a tight corner!" One

[1] There is ample proof that the western coast of the long island has been sinking since the end of the Glacial period. Thus, masses of peat are frequently dragged up by the anchors of fishing vessels.

The Kilt Rock, Skye

of Ketil's descendants married "Alfdis the Barra-woman": and
about 874 we read of a naval victory gained at Barra by Onund
Wooden Leg over Cerball, King ·of Ossory. But it would far
exceed the limits of this introductory sketch to pursue further
the numerous and colourful references to the Northern Hebrides
in the Sagas. By the year 1100 the powerful Norwegian monarch,
Magnus Bareleg, had reduced the endemic anarchy to some sort
of order, and had established an effective Norse sovereignty over
the Hebrides, which lasted until the Treaty of Perth in 1266. As
a result of that Treaty, "Man, already under English ecclesiastical
influence, gravitated into the power of England; and the Hebrides
were absorbed, though by a process so slow that it was not
completed before the Union of the Crowns, into the Kingdom
of Scotland."[1]

Neither is it necessary here to follow the growth of the famous
Lordship of the Isles, the successor of Somerled's Kingdom; its
long and inveterate struggle with the Stewart kings, until its final
destruction by James IV in 1493;[2] the rise to power in the resultant
void of the great House of Campbell, and its ruthless treatment
of all rival clans; the salutary measures of James VI and Charles I,
unhappily brought to naught by the outbreak of the Civil Wars;
and the final absorption of the Hebrides in the British body politic,
with all that this has meant in gain and loss, after the two Jacobite
risings in the eighteenth century.

The hundred years that followed the "Forty-five" were a period
of great distress in the Northern Hebrides—marked successively
by the growth of the population, after the abolition of clan warfare, beyond the means of subsistence; the failure of the kelp
industry and the great potato famine of 1846–7; the clearances
enforced in the interest of sheep farming, and the resultant mass
emigration, which has left undying bitterness in the hearts both
of the exiles and their descendants, and of those who remained
behind; the oppression caused by the resident factors of absentee
landlords; and last but not least, the social strains and discontents
bred by two World Wars. Yet much has been done, by successive
governments, of whatever political colour, to redeem the lot
of the islanders; and it may be said that, in not a few respects,
their prospects are brightening. Depopulation, however, persists,

[1] Lindsay Scott, *ut supra*, p. 210.
[2] The title is now vested in the eldest son of the sovereign, i.e. the Prince of
Wales, who in Scotland is Duke of Rothesay and Lord of the Isles.

2

Mingary Castle, Argyllshire

though in the Long Island it is partly masked by the steady growth of Stornoway. Moreover, emigration and war result inevitably in an ageing community, though this is less evident in the Roman Catholic islands, where families tend to be larger. But the broad trend, throughout the Hebrides, is that the "age pyramid" becomes unbalanced.

The population of the islands must always remain one of farmers, crofters, and fishermen. All of them suffer, in various ways, from distance from their markets and the cost of transport: though it is fair to say that motor-vessel services, piers and roads, as well as air transport, have all been much improved since the last War; and the process continues. Arable farming is of minor consequence: most of the cultivated land is given over to rough pasture for sheep and beef or dairy cattle.

Most of the peasantry are crofters, working small-holdings, say from five to eight acres, apart from the hill-moor or grazing land held in common by the township, and apportioned in the annual "souming". The history of crofting in the Hebrides, and of the various efforts made by government intervention to place it on a sound economic basis, is a fascinating one. The problem seems indeed intractable, and has been well described as one of "economic failure redeemed by social fortitude". Crofters near Stornoway can find work in the town. Both Skye and Lewis are suffering from a decline in crofting, but both islands may find employment in the development of North Sea oil.

Fishing, including lobster fishing, still helps to support the economy of the Hebrides; and in recent years the activities of the Forestry Commission, particularly in Skye, have sounded a note of promise. Perhaps the chief hope for the future lies in tourism—though this is hampered by the Sabbatarian prejudices of the islanders. The earlier lack of accommodation has been improved by considerable increase in the number of hotels, boarding houses and private houses offering accommodation, licensed camping sites, some with caravans to let. Shooting, angling, and mountaineering each bring a further quota of seasonal visitors to the islands.

Crofting having been for ages the chief occupation of the islanders, the main feature of man's devising in the Hebridean scene has been the dwellings of the crofters. These were the famous "black houses", now fast on the way out: for the modern crofter is now being housed, with government aid, in neat two-storeyed cottages, with "all mod. cons.", including windows that open; and the old "black house" is either left to ruin, or sometimes is used as a byre or peat store. Nevertheless, a fair number are in occupation, while one or two are being maintained as "period pieces". It therefore seems desirable to describe, in some detail, the Hebridean "black house".

The typical "black house", then, is oblong in plan, with rounded or "bull-nosed" corners. This no doubt is principally due to the fact that it is built out of field gatherings, mostly glacial boulders, and not out of quarried stones with sharp angles. Partly, however, the reason may be that the rounded angles do not offer the same resistance to the raving Hebridean gales, and so spare the house a good deal of shaking. The house may be as much as fifty feet by twelve feet in interior dimensions. The walls, usually built with a certain degree of inward slope or "batter", are constructed with an outer and inner boulder facing, the space between being packed with earth and small stones. Mortar is never used, but the interstices in the outer facing may be packed with moss. Not seldom the wall-face is lime-washed: it then contrasts pleasantly with the pale yellow thatch. Upon an average, the walls are from four to six feet thick, and about six feet in height. There are no gables, the ends of the thatched roof being "hipped"—that is, they slope inwards to the roof-ridge. The roof rests upon the inner edge of the wall, so that a man may scramble around it when the thatch requires repair or renewal. Sometimes this wall-head platform carries a bright array of wilding flowers. The timber couples are composed in the main of driftwood. The thatch is of bent grass, bracken or heather—more rarely of straw. It is kept in position by heather ropes weighted with stones and slung over the building, sometimes also by worn-out fishing nets—pegged down into the wall-heads, it may be with splints of bone. Great care is taken in the laying of the thatch. It is usually made in two thicknesses. Regularly in the summer season the thatching is renewed. First the outer layer is removed with great care, and spread out on the ground. Then the inner layer is stripped out; and since this is heavily impregnated with peat soot, it is used as manure. The old upper layer is then replaced as the lower, and a new upper layer of fresh thatch laid over it.[1] The outer layer, when it is of straw, is made from

[1] In the Long Isle, tweeds were sometimes dried on the roof.

barley stems not cut, but pulled up and laid with their roots nearest the roof-ridge. This gives them an anchorage.

The only chimney is a hole in the thatch. It is not directly over the hearth below, lest rain should put out the fire. In the outer walls the windows are few and narrow, such as can be closed by a single plate of glass. This is deeply sunk in the wall, whose exterior sides may be whitened. Occasionally there may be a window in the roof.

Inside, in the most primitive "black houses" no partition will be found. The animals occupy one end, the crofter's family the other, both using the one and only door. For obvious reasons, the house is built on a slope, and the lower half is assigned to the "cattle beasts"—not seldom, to the crofter's only cow. Alternatively the floor may be laid at two levels. In the lower part the dung is allowed to accumulate until the spring. The open rafters above afford a lodgment for the poultry. The floor of both sections of the house is made of clay trodden hard. Near the centre is the open circular stone hearth, laid in clay, from which the acrid, though fragrant, peat smoke escapes either through the chimney above, or perhaps as much by the door. Inevitably, the interior of the house is covered with a fine patina of soot, and the older inmates tend to acquire ebon complexions. The fire is kept burning night and day, so that the house is always warm. From the rafter immediately above the hearth, the cooking pot is suspended over the fire by an iron chain. The furniture is home made, simple and rude, and the family sleep in box beds.

Such was the Hebridean "black house" in its most primitive stage. Latterly, however, practically all of them had been sub-divided by a rough wooden partition, shutting off the byre from the living-room. These partitions were seldom carried up into the rafters. A still later refinement was to provide a separate byre, also built "black house" fashion. In the dwelling house, the central hearth gave place to fireplaces in each end, with stone chimneys, to a height less than that of the roof-ridge, and some-times crowned with an inverted pail with the bottom knocked out, or even by a chimney can. There was loss as well as gain in this refinement, since the traditional central hearth was the focus round which the crofting family and their friends gathered for their winter "socials", known as *ceilidh*, which have been the means of preserving so much of immemorial Hebridean folk lore and poetry.

Beside the "black house" was usually a small, untidy patch of garden; and hard by was the peat stack. This was a work of art, built with great skill, in the form of an upturned boat—curiously resembling in profile the earliest stone-built Christian churches in Ireland. In both cases, the shape was dictated by the need to throw off the wet in a rainy climate. It may, however, here be remarked that peat-cutting is on the decline in the Hebrides. It is a laborious process; the crofters are not as a class energetic; and other forms of fuel are now readily available.

I have tried to give a picture of these Hebridean houses in their most primitive form, which has been claimed to be "the simplest surviving homestead in Western Europe". Latterly, however, with the steady if slow rise in the crofters' standard of life, and increased contact with the outer world—mainly owing to the fact that the younger members of the community sought a living—or at least part-time employment—on the mainland, many improvements and additions to domestic comfort have gradually been introduced. Dark, leaky, smoky and grimy, the "black houses" may always have been, but it is an utter mistake to imagine that they housed a squalid or degraded population. Nor was their outer aspect "ugly and dwarfish", as a writer who ought to have known better once styled them. On the contrary, they chimed in more sweetly with the landscape than the trim white cottages which have supplanted them. Insanitary doubtless they were, yet they bred, upon the whole, a healthy population, and there are many recorded instances of crofters living to a great age. In former days, small-pox, typhoid and more recently tuberculosis, were the chief scourges of the crofting community.

How surprisingly the interior of a "black house" could belie its outward aspect will be understood from an experience of my own, more than thirty years ago. Though doubtless exceptional, I have no reason to believe it was unique.

I was tramping in a remote, desolate corner of Skye. The day was hot, and I thirsted. Presently, tucked away in an alcove of the rocky moorland, I came across a "black house". Immediately I was struck by its unusually trig appearance. Beside it were the inevitable, architectural peat stack and a neat little garden; also a well, with a large wooden bucket bespeaking a plenitude of water. So I knocked at the door of the "black house" to beg a drink. It was promptly opened by a middle-aged woman, doubtless the crofter's wife. She was neatly dressed and scrupulously clean: her features, though somewhat darkened by peat reek, were good, and I remember that she had white teeth and a pair of intelligent eyes. With true Highland courtesy she bade me indoors, offered a chair, and set before me, not water, but a large tumbler of delicious milk, with a noble topping of cream.

As we talked—she in good English, with a charming Hebridean lilt—I looked round the room. The house was divided by a partition, neatly covered with some stuff that looked to me like scrim. This partition rose into the rafters. Doubtless the room beyond, which I did not enter, will have been the kitchen. The stone walls of the living-room, where exposed, were white-washed; so were the rafters. In the gable was a good fireplace, with the embers of a peat fire. Along the back wall was a box bed, neatly fashioned. The furniture was simple, but good; a table, chairs, and by the fire an armchair and a stool. In a window bay stood an Aladdin lamp.

A number of books lay around, some in fresh dust jackets; also a pile of copies of the *Illustrated London News*. What struck me most of all was a handsome wireless set. When I expressed surprise at finding these refinements in a remote crofter's house in Vaternish, my kind hostess explained to me that her son was an officer in the merchant navy, and that he had brought these gifts home on various occasions when on leave. So I gave her my card, and asked her to tell her son, if his boat ever brought him to Aberdeen, to be sure to give me the chance of returning his mother's hospitality. The crofter may wander far afield, but invariably he returns to his home; and as often as not he retires there.

Such having been for centuries the traditional homes of the Hebridean crofters, what shall we say about the people? What sort of character has been bred in them by generations of life in such surroundings, amid such a climate and such scenery, and under such toilsome conditions?

These questions are not easy to answer, owing to the inbred reserve and indeed suspicion of the crofter, and to some extent still by the language difficulty.

The first thing that will strike a visitor who makes a serious effort to get in touch with the people in their own homes, or at least in their rural surroundings, is a certain sense of melancholy. How far this is due to generations of life in an unsympathetic climate, to long hours of monotonous toil, to what until recent years was a seemingly endless wrestle with poverty, I shall not presume to guess. How far the gloomy character of their narrow religious faith, in the Calvinistic islands at least, is responsible— whether indeed it is cause or effect—is an equally difficult question: for the beliefs of the early Christian Celts embodied a strong tendency to dwell upon the terrible, upon divine retribution rather than divine mercy, as will be conceded by all who have studied the life and recorded utterances of St Columba.[1]

Perhaps also to the mild humid climate of the Hebrides may be ascribed the indolence which has often been charged against the natives. This appears the more likely since the islanders, when away from their native scenes, have displayed remarkable energy, alike in war and peace. Of their easy-going habits at home there can be no doubt. Everyone has heard of the crofter's prayer:

> O that the peats would cut themselves,
> The fish shump on the shore,
> And that we all in bed might lie
> For aye and evermore!

Somebody once uncharitably remarked that in the Hebrides it takes two men to do one man's work, with two others to look on! Whatever may be the truth in this gibe, I am much afraid that it could nowadays be applied, with equal justice or injustice, to other parts of Britain.

Combined with this indolence is a stubborn unreasoning conservatism and resistance to improvements, such as in Lewis even Viscount Leverhulme's vision, force and lavishness failed to master. Many other well-meant attempts to ameliorate the crofters' lot, before and since, have foundered upon the same rock.

A fourth weakness of the Hebridean character which may be at least in part ascribed to the climate, is intemperance. Upon this a great deal has been written—much of it exaggerated and jaundiced. Yet there can be no doubt, from an amplitude of evidence, that for centuries over-addiction to strong waters has been a curse of the Highlanders. The rabid teetotalism of too many of the clergy has tended to drive this vice underground, rather than to diminish it. But nowadays things are on the mend. The rise in

---

[1] On this matter reference may be made to my *The Historical Saint Columba*, 3rd ed. (1963), pp. 54-5, 64-5.

the crofter's well-being; the improvement in his material surroundings; the fact that now he has many other things on which
to spend his money and his leisure—motor-cars, wireless, tele-
vision, the picture house, and all the rest; the growth in education;
increasing contacts with an outer world which has wider satis-
factions to offer—all these things are working, slowly yet surely,
with beneficent effect. The disgraceful scenes at pierhead or in
pub, the orgies that formerly accompanied funerals—such ex-
cesses, which have been described with too much gusto, and no
doubt with equal exaggeration, by certain writers on the Hebrides,
can no longer be regarded as a characteristic of insular society.

Strange though the idea may sound, it has been seriously con-
tended that more ill health has in recent times been caused in the
island by tea drinking than by the whisky bottle. The crofts being
small, the crofter never works far from his home. Here his wife
keeps a tea kettle continually on the boil, and the thirsty crofter
comes in repeatedly for his "cuppie". Thus each day he imbibes
a large amount of tannic acid; and I have heard a doctor, prac-
tising in Skye, declare that much digestive disturbance, and even
serious illness, results from this over-indulgence.

It has been said that the crofter is "slim"; and certainly, like
most of us, he has a shrewd eye to his own advantage. Much of
what has been accounted lack of candour is doubtless due to the
inborn courtesy of the Celt, which leads him to shrink from giving
an unpleasant answer. Very properly, the crofter keeps to himself
his own affairs: yet rumour has it, that, with the general improvement of crofting conditions, and the generous subvention handed
out by the State, not a few members of the crofting community
could show a surprising bank balance.

Habitual courtesy to strangers:[1] a complete lack of class-
consciousness; heartiness in friendship: patience and profound
endurance in adversity—these we must salute as the solid virtues
of the islander. Polite he is almost invariably, yet rarely or never
servile. The crofter enjoys fixity of tenure, and a secure if modest
living. His isolation, and difficulty of access to his markets, has
been much abated by the advent of the tradesman's van, the
travelling shop, the lorry and the tractor. What he makes from

[1] Samuel Johnson was right in saying that "civility seems part of the national
character of Highlanders". In our rough mannerless age, let no one think that
the habitual courtesy to strangers which one meets in the Hebrides is a mere
superficial virtue.

his croft he can now amplify from side occupations. He is a member of a closely-knit society, with its own standards, rules and obligations; and, as such he feels he has a stake in the country. His life may seem to us monotonous, but not more so than that of countless toilers in our city factories. If he does not make as much as the artisan with a militant union behind him, or the opportunity of increasing his earnings by overtime, on the other hand his wants are fewer; and, to a much larger extent than the urban worker, he is master of his own time. Instead of being thirled to a single monotonous technical process, he derives creative satisfaction from what has been well described as "a wide range of simple skills". In the two great wars of our century, the crofters of the Hebrides have served their country with honour, and not seldom with glory, on lands and waters far remote from their native islands. What wonder, therefore, that the Highland crofter of today is in no respect inclined to undervalue himself? And no student of the crofting community in the Hebrides can deny it, as a whole, the credit of an indomitable will to live.

The rhythm of the crofter's life varies much between the Inner and the Outer Hebrides, and indeed from island to island. Thus in the Long Island, as we shall find, weaving has provided an important additional source of income. The menfolk usually ply it during the interval between sowing and harvest. Fishing, including lobster fishing, though far less important than in former times, is still a substantial industry in Lewis and Harris—particularly in crofting communities which have the good luck to be sited on deep sea-lochs. In fact, it may well be suspected that the opportunities for fishing have dictated the choice of site for many such littoral townships. Freshwater fishing, deer-stalking, and shooting (hares and grouse) are not normally activities of the crofter's life, except if he be a poacher; but (as noted above, p. 18) they provide some ancillary employment during the sporting season. As to his agricultural economy, the Hebridean crofter tends to rely more and more on grass grown for grazing, and less and less on agriculture. Enormous quantities of white bread are imported all the year round from Glasgow; and the insular housewife is fully aware of the variety and range of modern tinned and potted foods. As the crofter thus depends more and more upon external sources of supply, he is the more liable to inconvenience, even hardship, if this be interrupted by stress of weather.

Many observers have commented upon the relative backwardness of the Hebridean crofters, as compared with the peasantry of Denmark, and Rogaland and Hordaland in south-western Norway, where the physical conditions are much the same. Probably more than one reason has contributed to this unfavourable contrast. Something doubtless must be ascribed to the habitual indolence of the Gael. Then the Hebrides are far more remote from the great industrial centres of Britain, and therefore could not share fully in the enormous advances which characterized British agriculture after the Napoleonic Wars. Still further back in time, we must never forget how the Gaelic spirit was broken by the ruthless policy of the Hanoverian government after the Forty-five. The destruction of the clan system, to which the whole Hebridean society was geared, bore along with itself consequences extending far beyond the field of politics.

In no respect, perhaps, has the progressive improvement in the crofter's lot been more evident than in the easing of woman's burden. Apart from the inevitable function of child-bearing, the Hebridean woman of an older generation was mainly responsible for the gross labour of cutting the peat, which in former days was the chief source of fuel. Cut during the fine months of May and June, the peat was stacked till it dried, and then the women folk had to load it into creels or long baskets, to be born on their backs down to the peat store in the croft. Apart from the fact that less and less peat is now being cut, improved roads and motor transport, including tractors, enable the peat to be carted down to the roadside, and so to the crofter's peat stack. In fishing communities, the women would help to get the nets ready, bait the lines and dry the fish. Weaving and basket making filled in the long winter evenings. As for the burden of maternity, the unfailing helpfulness of neighbours, in a crofting township, deserves warm recognition.

One very famous implement of crofting tillage has now entirely disappeared from the Hebrides. This is the *cas chrom* or foot plough, now only to be seen in Highland folk-museums, or in the hands of those who love to collect "byegones". Nearly two hundred years ago, that acute observer, wise old Samuel Johnson, described this remarkable tool of primitive husbandry in language that could not be bettered. Writing about the crofters of Skye, he says:

Their corn grounds often lie in such intricacies among the craggs, that there is no room for the action of a team and plow. The soil is then turned up by manual labour, with an instrument called a crooked spade, of a form and weight which to me appeared very incommodious, and would perhaps be soon improved in a country where workmen could be easily found and easily paid. It has a narrow blade of iron fixed to a long and heavy piece of wood, which must have, about a foot and a half above the iron, a knee or flexure with the angle downwards. When the farmer encounters a stone which is the great impediment of his operations, he drives the blade under it, and bringing the knee or angle to the ground, has in the long handle a very forcible lever.

The one and only time I saw the *cas chrom* in operation was in Skye, between the two wars. This one had a rest for the foot. Upon ground such as Johnson describes, it seemed to me to do its job quite effectively. But as early as 1549, Dean Monro records that pony-drawn ploughs were in use in the less rugged areas of Lewis. Four ponies abreast were required to haul the plough; and of course the work was a combined operation by a crofting team. The plough was preceded by a "reestle", a kind of primitive harrow, which required a couple of ponies to drag it.

Until well into the nineteenth century, the middle tier of the social pyramid in the Hebrides was formed by the tacksman. Though now extinct, this remarkable class has left an enduring imprint upon the Hebridean economy, and *ethos*. Here again, we may turn to Samuel Johnson for an excellent introduction:

Next in dignity to the Laird is the Tacksman: a large taker or lease-holder of land, of which he keeps part, as a domain, in his own hand, and lets part to under tenants. The Tacksman is necessarily a man capable of securing to the Laird the whole rent, and is commonly a collateral relation. These tacks, or subordinate possessions, were long considered as hereditary, and the occupant was distinguished by the name of the place at which he resided. He held a middle station, by which the highest and the lowest orders were connected. He paid rent and reverence to the Laird, and received them from the tenants. This tenure still subsists, with its original operation, but not with the primitive stability. Since the islanders, no longer content to live, have learned the desire of growing rich, an ancient dependent is in danger of giving way to a higher bidder, at the expense of domestick dignity and hereditary power.

The stranger, whose money buys him preference, considers himself as paying for all that he has, and is indifferent about the Laird's honour or safety. The commodiousness of money is indeed great; but there are some advantages which money cannot buy, and which therefore no wise man will by the love of money be tempted to forego.

In the pages of Johnson's Journal and Boswell's Tour we get a vivid portrait of the Skye tacksmen. We see them living well and on the whole wisely. If they over-ate and over-drank, that was the fashion of "gentlemen farmers" all over Britain in the eighteenth century. As a class they were well educated, and not seldom were men of culture, whose houses contained good books. Many were retired officers, and had seen service overseas. Of the Highlanders who volunteered for the American War, the tacksmen had, in many cases, been the natural and very gallant leaders. They continued such in the Highland regiments during the Napoleonic Wars. Possessed of a natural ease of manners, they could meet on equal terms the aristocrat or the man of learning: moreover, they lived in intimate patriarchal contact with their crofters. Their ladies were equally *salonfähig*, and both Johnson and Boswell have testified to their astonishment at the generous and refined hostmanship which they enjoyed in tacksmen's houses.

With the insight of a powerful and penetrating mind, Johnson clearly perceived the essential part which the tacksmen played in Hebridean society as he found it:

As the mind must govern the hands, so in every society the man of intelligence must direct the man of labour. If the Tacksmen be taken away, the Hebrides must in their present state be given up to grossness and ignorance; the tenant, for want of instruction, will be unskilful, and for want of admonition will be negligent. The Laird in these wide estates, which often consist of islands remote from one another, cannot extend his personal influence to all his tenants; and the steward having no dignity annexed to his character, can have little authority among men taught to pay reverence only to birth, and who regard the Tacksman as their hereditary superior; nor can the steward have equal zeal for the prosperity of an estate profitable only to the Laird, with the Tacksman, who has the Laird's income involved in his own.

The only gentlemen in the Islands are the Lairds, the Tacksmen, and the Ministers, who frequently improve their livings by becoming farmers. If the Tacksman be banished, who will be left to impart knowledge, or impress civility? The Laird must always be at a distance from the greater part of his lands; and if he resides at all upon them, must drag his days in solitude, having no longer either a friend or companion; he will therefore depart to some more comfortable residence, and leave the tenants to the wisdom and mercy of the factor.

How thoroughly this prophecy of the old English *savant* was to be fulfilled, the later history of the Hebrides would amply show. Of course there were bad as well as good tacksmen, as the folk traditions of the Hebridean crofters bear ample testimony: but such records of ancient grievances are as nothing to the hatred expressed, reasonably or unreasonably, to the successor of the tacksman, the factor of an absent laird. Most of the grudge of the crofters against the tacksmen consists in the fact that they extracted rents not only in kind and in money (where money was available) but also in service; and forced labour is never popular.

We have seen that in Johnson's time the tacksman system was in the decline in Skye. In the Outer Isles it had long been undergoing a slow, but cumulatively radical and deleterious transformation. Many of the "Fife Adventurers", introduced to Lewis by the policy of James VI, took up their position in the island economy as tacksmen: while the Seaforth Mackenzies, when they replaced the "Fifers", introduced many of their clansmen in the same capacity. Thus the ancient function of the tacksman as a link between the chief and the crofters, was from the early seventeenth century undergoing a process of slow attrition. In Lewis in particular, the stranger tacksmen introduced by the Crown and the Seaforths in the seventeenth century, tended to live a life apart from the native crofters. Yet the deeper its roots in the soil, the more permanent is a community. Hence about Lewis a distinguished modern geographer has well remarked that "the tacksmen were to pass away, as many of them had originally come, at the desire of a mainland lord, and the lord, in his turn, was to leave: but the small peasantry of immemorial stock still hold and work their land."[1] All over the Hebrides, the successor of the tacksman is now the farmer—not seldom the farmer-owner, and more often than not of Lowland stock. But the policy of Government has been to break up farms into crofts; and we shall see that it was on this point that Viscount Leverhulme's plans for a revival of prosperity in Lewis foundered.

[1] Arthur Geddes, *Lewis and Harris*, p. 119.

At the apex of the social pyramid in the Hebrides were the clan chiefs or lairds. Alas! these have now well nigh disappeared, save for the Chief of the Clan Macleod at Dunvegan, The Macneil of Barra at Kisimul, and Lord Macdonald at Armadale. Of people living it is seemly to speak with reserve: yet no one conversant with the Hebrides today would deny that all of these three chiefs of clans have, in their own way, done their duty not only to their tenants and clansmen, but to the wider interests of the Scottish Highlands.

II

ARDNAMURCHAN: THE PORTAL
OF THE NORTHERN HEBRIDES

We have seen that in 1156 that tremendous character, Somerled, after a naval victory over his suzerain, Godred, the Norse King of Man and the Isles, imposed upon him a partition of his domains. Under this agreement, the islands south of the Point of Ardnamurchan were ceded to Somerled, while the Northern Hebrides remained under the nominal rule of the King of Man. By this astute move, Somerled not only secured for himself the larger and more fertile of the Hebrid Isles: he also divided the realm of the King of Man; and, in effect, dealt the death-blow to an insular domain that had extended from the Calf of Man to the Butt of Lewis, and had included the mainland peninsula of Kintyre.

It is obvious that, as a result of this partition, the noble peninsula of Ardnamurchan, the Point of which is the most westerly headland of the British mainland, acquired a unique strategic importance, which indeed it retained until the seventeenth century. It completely dominated the long Sound of Mull, the *fauces angustissimae portus* of the Northern Hebrides—the quickest and safest channel between the Southern and Northern Islands. Controlling this sea-passage, Somerled and his successors were in a position either to launch a further enterprise upon the northern half of Godred's dominions, or to ward off any attack from the north, whether by Godred or by his superior, the King of Norway. For this reason, the Ardnamurchan peninsula was secured by two early stone castles, Mingary and Tioram. A sixteenth-century official report speaks of

ane Ness passand southwest fra the lands of Ardmwrche, quhilk Ness is called Romwrche [Point of Ardnamurchan], and divides thir haill Iles in twa; viz. in South and North Iles, viz. the Iles of Ila and Mule with thair saids pertinents, lyand fra the said Ness to the South and the Iles of Lewis and Sky to the North.

Not only is the Ardnamurchan peninsula thus closely linked in history with the Northern Hebrides, but geologically it is intimately associated with the neighbouring Small Isles and Skye. In both senses it is thus the springboard of our insular investigation; and hence it is appropriate now to glance, very briefly, at one of the most remarkable features of the Hebridean coastland, which belongs as truly to the Northern Isles as the peninsula of Kintyre has always been reckoned part of the Southern.

Ardnamurchan measures about 16 miles in length and some 7 miles in greatest breadth. The interior forms a range of bare or barren hills, culminating in Ben Hiant (1,729 feet). The coasts are rugged and rocky, though not in general rising into very lofty cliffs. On the south side, near the western end, is the important haven of Kilchoan, from early days a port of call, and one of the places where cattle droves from the Hebrides were landed on the mainland. Between the coast and the hills there is much good arable land, particularly round Kilchoan, and on the north side about Achateny and Sanna. Parts of the peninsula are finely wooded, for example round the modern Glenborrodale Castle and between Salen and Strontian.

Geologically, Ardnamurchan is classic country. Its eastern portion consists of metamorphic rocks belonging to the Moine Schists—differing from, perhaps later in date, than, the Lewisian gneiss which we shall find so amply developed in the Outer Isles. But the western portion or snout of the peninsula consists of a vast and highly complex suite of igneous rocks, the basal wreck or dissected roots of one of those giant volcanoes which spewed out their incandescent contents along what is now the Atlantic seaboard of Scotland in Eocene times, some fifty to seventy million years ago. When we come to Skye we shall have to look in some detail at this stupendous outburst of igneous activity—perhaps the grandest such episode in the ascertained geological history of Europe. Here it must suffice to say that the Ardnamurchan volcano comprised three successive centres of extrusion, and that, as we shall find in Skye, and again in St Kilda, basic magmas tended to be succeeded by more acid materials.

It has been computed that the internal walls of the Ardnamurchan craters were sometimes at least 1,000 feet in height. The agglomerate which fills one of these ancient vents is exposed on the southern sea-front in the bold bluff, rising to a height of some

900 feet, known as Maclean's Nose, thus presenting us in effect with a cast of the ancient crater.

As in Skye and the Shiant Islands, this vast volcanic pile has sealed up, and therefore protected from denudation, an interesting suite of Mesozoic rocks, Triassic and Jurassic, which are now exposed along the coasts. In places these sedimentary deposits are rich in fossils.

The Ardnamurchan volcano is easily accessible. It can be thoroughly explored without undue physical exertion; and it has been the subject of an exhaustive and masterly Memoir of H.M. Geological Survey.[1] Complicated though it may appear on first study of the coloured map, its basic structure is essentially simple. It is therefore an admirable subject for the amateur geologist to commence his study of Tertiary vulcanicity in the Hebrides, prior to moving on to the much more austere and arduous investigation of the Cuillins.

Before leaving this fascinating subject of the geology of Ardnamurchan, our amateur geologist is recommended to take his stand upon the eastern horn of Kilchoan Bay, and cast his eye westward over its gleaming waters to the opposite slopes, behind Ormsaigmore and Ormsaigbeg. His attention will at once be claimed by a conspicuous horizontal bench, cut out as it were in the hill slope all along the western side of the bay, at a height, fairly constantly maintained, of about 140 feet above high-tide level. This is not one of the post-glacial raised beaches so strikingly developed in many places around the coasts of Scotland. It is a Pliocene beach, as is evident from the absence of the gravels found on the post-glacial raised beaches at lower levels, and by its much higher degree of erosion. The same pre-glacial beach can be seen on the north side of Ardnamurchan, around Achateny.

The strategic importance of Ardnamurchan after Somerled's partition of the Hebrides is revealed by the fact that upon the peninsula there were in due course erected two stone-and-lime castles of the earliest type found on the western seaboard, and of which we shall encounter further examples at Dunvegan in Skye and Kisimul in Barra. Our two Ardnamurchan castles are of great

[1] *The Geology of Ardnamurchan, North-west Mull and Coll* (1930). See also J. E. Richey, British Regional Geology: *Scotland, the Tertiary Volcanic Districts*, 1935.

3

The Old Man of Storr, Skye

value, because in both the primary work has descended to our own time with surprisingly little alteration.

Mingary Castle occupies a position of great strategic importance. It stands on the south coast of Ardnamurchan, directly opposite the northern outlet of the Sound of Mull, and about six miles east of the Point. As we have noted, the principal channel of communication between the two divisions of the Hebrides, and between the Scottish mainland and the Northern Isles, lay through the Sound of Mull. It was commanded by two early castles of *enceinte*, at its southern end by Duart Castle in Mull, and at its northern end by Mingary in Ardnamurchan. With the reduction in 1222 by Alexander II of the great ancient Celtic province of Ergadia, which included the whole western seaboard from the Mull of Kintyre to Loch Broom, the royal power reached the Atlantic; and Dunstaffnage Castle at the mouth of the Great Glen was probably built as a springboard or advanced base for the projected conquest of the Hebrides, in preparing for which Alexander died in 1249 on the island of Kerrera. We can readily see how Mingary Castle fits in with the same policy:

> From where Mingarry, sternly placed,
> O'erawes the woodland and the waste,
> To where Dunstaffnage hears the raging
> Of Connal with his rocks engaging.

The vital Sound of Mull was thus held firmly in the grip of mainland power. The choice of site for Castle Tioram, on its tidal islet in romantic Loch Moidart, is less immediately apparent. But it commands an ancient route from Strontian along upper Loch Sunart to Salen, and so over the head of Loch Moidart—a route much later used in the reverse direction by some at least of the drovers from the Small Isles. The continued importance of both castles is shown by the part which they played in "Colkitto" Macdonald's sea-borne invasion in 1644, and by the fact that both were garrisoned by the Hanoverian Government during the Jacobite period.

This is not the place to embark upon any detailed description of Mingary Castle and Castle Tioram—particularly as I have fully discussed them elsewhere,[1] and they have also been considered in their context by Mr Stewart Cruden in his standard book on *The*

[1] See *Trans. Glasg. Archaeol. Soc.*, n.s., vol. XIII (1954), pp. 70–90.

Scottish Castle. In both, the primary feature is the great ring wall of *enceinte*, adjusted to the contours of the rock site, and thereby precluded from such sophistications as flanking towers. Duart, mentioned above, falls into the same category; and we shall see it again at Dunvegan and Kisimul. As at Kisimul, Mingary and Tioram retain the provision, usual in the twelfth and thirteenth centuries, for defending the curtain from timber oversailing war-heads. Since the restoration of Kisimul Castle has inevitably ob-scured to some extent these features, the two Ardnamurchan castles are of all the greater value. At Mingary, original lancet windows, in two places paired, leave us in no doubt as to the First Pointed date of the castle.

The principal ancient ecclesiastical site in Ardnamurchan is Kilchoan, St Congan's Church. St Congan was a son of the King of Leinster, and his sister was the famous Caintegern or Kenti-gerna, the saint of Loch Lomond, and mother of St Fillan. She died in 734, a date which fixes the period of St Congan. With his sister and her three sons and accompanied by other missionaries, he established himself at Lochalsh in Wester Ross, where two ancient church sites, Kilchoan and Kilillan, still preserve the names of St Congan and St Fillan respectively. From this centre the missionary activities of St Congan spread over the western main-land and the isles, as recorded by his church sites still existing in Islay at Loch Melfort; in Ardnamurchan; in Knoydart; in Skye; and in North Uist. But the lure of the rich and populous eastern plains of Pictland attracted him as it had attracted St Moluag, St Maelrubha, and other Irish missionaries of whom we shall read later on in this book. Thus we have St Congan's Church at Kiltearn in Easter Ross, and the more famous monastery which he founded at Turriff on the Deveron, one of the most important centres of Celtic Christianity betwixt Dee and Spey.

The ruined church of Kilchoan dates only from 1763; the pre-sent parish church from 1831. But in the kirkyard are at least two grave-slabs of the characteristic West Highland type, of which we shall encounter other examples when we cross over to the Isles. One displays a galley masted and with furled sails, along with the figure of a mailed warrior; beautiful zoomorphic enrichment; and, as often on the monuments, the great two-handed sword, or claymore, as the central feature of the composition. The other

slab, much worn, shows a floriated cross, the usual central claymore, beast forms, and at the base a galley.[1]

East of Kilchoan is *Camus nan Geall*, with the site of St Columba's burial ground and well, with a much weathered standing
stone displaying a Celtic Cross. This site derives interest because
it brings us into touch with the earliest references to Ardnamurchan, found in Adamnan's Life of St Columba. In one place the
biographer records a prophetic revelation, dire in character, made
by the Saint to his companions "in the rough and rocky country
which is called Artdamuirchol". Even more vivid is the tale of the
Saint's encounter with Ioan, a prince of the royal line of Dalriada,
who had been persecuting a native of Ardnamurchan, Colman.
The latter, despite his poverty, had offered hospitality to Columba,
and had been duly rewarded by a miraculous increase in his cattle.
Apparently this new-found wealth had attracted the cupidity of
the Dalriadic princeling, who had descended upon Ardnamurchan
and plundered Colman's property. The story of how the indig-
nant saint, catching the riever *in flagrante delicto*, pursued him into
the green waves of the sea, assailing him with bitter curses, is described with great vigour, and the locality is explicitly identified
as "the place which is called in Irish Aithchambas Artmuirchal",
"the sharp bay of Ardnamurchan". We are not surprised to be
informed that the robber with his booty foundered between Mull
and Coll. Most important of all is the tale of how Columba bap-
tized an infant, Ligu Cen-calad, in Ardnamurchan—"where even
at this day there is a health-giving well called after St Columba".
More than likely this is the well at *Camus nan geall*. Close east of
Ardnamurchan lighthouse is *Eilean Chaluimchille*, which we may
well be inclined to recognize as a memorial of the great apostle's
presence in Ardnamurchan. Whatever we may think of the
miraculous character with which the actions of Columba are
invested by his credulous biographer, they give us our first and
vivid historical glimpses of Ardnamurchan.

Looking northward from the lofty lighthouse on the Point of
Ardnamurchan, if the weather is clear, a fine view is obtained of
the Small Isles, with the peaks of Skye behind. To these glamorous
islands of varied interest it is now incumbent upon us to move

[1] For these distinctive West Highland grave slabs reference may be made to
my *The Ancient Stones of Scotland* (1965) chap. xvii.

forwards. Meantime suffice it in conclusion to remark that Ardna-murchan lighthouse, 114 feet in height, and beautifully built of pink granite from the Ross of Mull, crowning as it does a stark cliff, has a revolving light which flashes twice every thirty seconds, casting forth a beam of 27,200 candle power. The sundial adjoin-ing records 25 minutes behind Greenwich time.

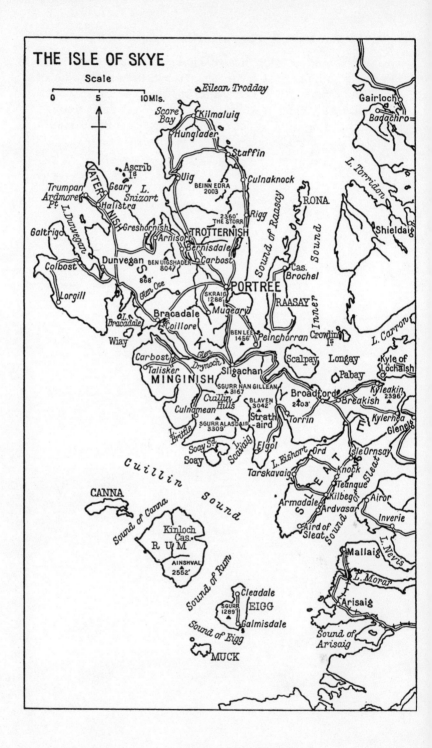

THE ISLE OF SKYE

Scale

0 ___ 5 ___ 10 Mls.

Eilean Trodday

Gairloch

Badachro

Score Bay

Kilmaluig

Hunglader

Staffin

Ascrib Is.

Uig

Culnaknock

L. Torridon

Trumpan
Ardmore Pt.

Geary

L. Snizort

BEINN EDRA 2003

Halistra

Rigg

RONA

Shieldaig

Greshornish

2360' THE STORR

Galtrigo

Arnisort

TROTTERNISH

L. Dunvegan

Bernisdale

Carbost

Sound of Raasay

Colbost

Dunvegan

BEN UIGSHADER 804'

Cas. Brochel

Inner Sound

Lorgill

868'

Glen Ose

PORTREE

SKRAIG 1288'

Mugeary

RAASAY

L. Carron

Bracadale

Coillore

Crowlin Is.

Kyle of Lochalsh

L. Bracadale

Wiay

BEN LEE 1456'

Peinchorran

Carbost

Glen Drynoch

Scalpay

Longay

Talisker

Sligachan

Pabay

MINGINISH

SGURR NAN GILLEAN 3167

Broadford

Kyleakin 2396'

Cuillin Hills

BLAVEN 3042'

2403'

Breakish

Culnamean

SGURR ALASDAIR 3309

Strath-aird

Torrin

Kylerhea

L. Brittle

Glenelg

Soay Sd.

L. Scavaig

Elgol

Ord

Isle Ornsay

S L E A T

Soay

L. Eishort

Tarskavaig

Knock

Teangue

Sound of Sleat

Cuillin   Sound

CANNA

Armadale

Kilbeg

Airor

Ardvasar

Inverie

Sound of Canna

Aird of Sleat

L. Nevis

Kinloch Cas.

R U M

Mallaig

AINSHVAL 2552'

Sound of Rum

L. Morar

Cleadale

Arisaig

SGURR 1289'

EIGG

Galmisdale

Sound of Eigg

Sound of Arisaig

MUCK

III

THE ISLE OF SKYE

Let them sing of the sunny south.
　Where the blue Aegean smiles,
But give to me the Scottish sea,
　That breaks round the Western Isles!
Jerusalem, Athens, and Rome,
　I would see them before I die!
But I'd rather not see any one of the three,
　Than be exiled for ever from Skye.
Lovest thou mountains great,
　Peaks to the clouds that soar,
Corrie and fell where eagles dwell,
　And cataracts dash evermore?
Lovest thou green grassy glades,
　By the sunshine sweetly kist,
Murmuring waves and echoing caves?
　Then go to the Isle of Mist!

The Island of Skye—the "Misty Isle" as it has long been called; the
"isle of kind and loyal hearts", as the late King George VI described it when he visited Skye, as Duke of York, in 1933—is the
largest but one of the Hebrides. Its main mass lies north-west and
south-east, running out at its broad upper end into the three long
promontories of Trotternish, Vaternish and Duirinish, divided
from each other by Loch Snizort and Loch Dunvegan. Midway
from the long western coast projects the squat mass of Minginish,
flanked by Loch Bracadale (with its inner arm, Loch Harport)
and Loch Scavaig. Beyond the latter the bold headland of Strathaird is isolated by Loch Slapin and Loch Eishort from the long
transverse butt of the island, known as Sleat and Strath, which in
shape is uncommonly like a gigantic fish's tail.

　The island is 49 miles in length. Its breadth varies from 7 to 25
miles. But owing to the irregularity of the coastline, and the great
number of fiord-like lochs, no part of the interior is as much as

5 miles from the sea. The total length of coast-line is over 900 miles.

Skye contains 690 square miles, most of which is moorland and mountain. Of the mountains, three main systems may be distinguished. The principal one is the grand group of the Cuillins, in the south-west, forming the base of Minginish. Without question these are the most magnificent of British mountains. From far and near their splintered jagged peaks of dark grey gabbro are the dominating element in the multiform profile of Skye. Their highest summit, the highest in the island, is Sgurr Alasdair (3,309 feet). But the best known is the grim point of Sgurr-nan-Gillean (3,167 feet), at the east end of the group, overlooking wild Glen Sligachan. By itself, on the other side of the Glen, but geologically belonging to the same formation, is Blaven (3,042 feet). Including it, the Cuillins contain fifteen summits of over 3,000 feet. The rock climbing afforded by these mountains is the most testing and dangerous in Britain.

Eastward from the Cuillins proper are the Red Cuillins or Red Hills. These are lower and smoother in outline, but impressive in their vast unresolved pyramidal masses of pink granophyre, blanketed with huge screes. The highest is Glamaig (2,537 feet).

The third mountain system in Skye is the long spine of swart basalt that forms the backbone of Trotternish, rising into the fantastic spires and pinnacles of the Storr (2,360 feet), and Quiraing (1,779 feet). Apart by themselves in Duirinish stand the two flat-topped basalt cakes of Healaval Mor (1,538 feet) and Healaval Beag (1,601 feet), more familiarly known as "MacLeod's Tables" (see page 69).

Geology is the womb of history: and so it is that through uncounted aeons of primeval time, and by gigantic processes of tectonic architecture, the profile and landscape of Skye, as I have sketched it in the foregoing paragraphs, and the human life that, for some four thousand years at least, has been evolved amid its stern mountains, its green valleys and its wine-dark moorlands, have been inexorably conditioned. In this long travail many tools have played their part. Some of these were violent, others gradual and, to our human eye, well-nigh imperceptible in their working. Such were the slow gathering of sediments in sheltered waters—the long upheaval of the earth's crust—the sudden cataclysm of volcanic outbreak—the more tranquil welling forth of mighty lava sheets—the subsidence of land surfaces beneath the weltering billows—the planing down of mountain masses by glaciers—the battering of coasts by wind and wave—the splintering of stubborn rock by frost—the scouring of the Highland streams.

To the geologist Skye is a *locus classicus*. The oldest rocks are found in Sleat. They consist of highly altered schists and gneisses—among the most ancient layers in the tough old hide of our mother earth. In the same peninsula are found the Torridonian sandstones, described above (p. 15). Primary rocks of the Cambrian series, partly fossiliferous, occur in Strath and elsewhere. The ancient life revealed by these fossils shows that in the Cambrian seas, which, possibly five hundred millions of years ago, covered those portions of what is now the Isle of Skye, there flourished sponges, shellfish, sea-worms, and—as the dominant forms of life in that primeval period—those strange creatures which the geologist terms trilobites; crustaceans that crawled about on the muddy sands of a shallow sea-floor. Trilobites could curl up like their remote descendants, the modern woodlouse; and their fossils are often found in this posture—as if they had rolled themselves up in the fright of their death-pang.

But it is at a much later period in the vast chronology of the geological record—in the Jurassic epoch, perhaps one hundred and fifty million years ago, according to the latest computations—that we first obtain a fairly clear picture of conditions in what is now Skye. The Jurassic strata of Strathaird, Broadford and Trotternish have yielded many characteristic fossils. These enable us to picture the life of that ancient time against the background of what is otherwise known about the Jurassic stage in the evolution of our globe. During that epoch, Skye formed the bed of a narrow arm of an inshore sea between two continental masses, one of which occupied much of the present area of the North Sea, Scandinavia, and the Baltic, while the other covered part of the North Atlantic. Midway in this sea there was a large island which included most of the present Scotland and extended as far south as the Pennine range. In the sheltered and shallow brackish waters that washed the western shores of this island, beds of limestone, shale and sandstone were laid down; and in these beds are entombed the remains of the denizens of that ancient sea. The climate of Britain was then sub-tropical—hot and damp. Dense forests of tree-fern, giant horse-tails, conifers and cycads overspread the land. Of the animal kingdom huge reptiles were the lords. The first birds were just evolving, and also the earliest mammals—small marsupials, no larger than a rat or a hedgehog. In the warm waters flourished a marine fauna of amazing variety and abundance.

Thousands of centuries passed away. Gradually, very gradually, the crust of the earth was elevated. The waters flowed away, and the beds of sandstone and limestone emerged as solid land. Atmospheric erosion then set in, and continued over an immense lapse of time, so that many of the upper Jurassic strata were removed. At least one further period of shallow subsidence followed, accompanied by desert conditions on the land that escaped being drowned. Then another upheaval on a grand scale took place. Probably as a result of the stresses caused by these tremendous crustal movements, volcanic activity, of titanic dimensions, broke out over an area extending from Britain to Greenland. The eruptions continued during an enormous number of centuries, and ceased (so far as Britain is concerned) probably some forty million years ago, about the close of the Eocene period—though the last lingering efforts of that ancient plutonic convulsion still manifest themselves today in Iceland. Along the western coast of Scotland— in Arran, in Mull, in Ardnamurchan, in Rum and in Skye—the geologist has recognized the basal wrecks of a chain of vast volcanoes of that early time. From these five vents, and others now drowned beneath the Atlantic, as well as from minor craters such as those at Kilchrist and Broadford in Skye, were outpoured, probably quite tranquilly, the enormous flows of lava that now form the basalt sheets and terraces of the Hebrides. In Skye, some 425 square miles of country are covered by these plateau basalts; and despite millions of years of denudation, they remain to a total thickness of 2,000 feet. In Mull, there survives a thickness of no less than 6,000 feet of basaltic lavas: here also the central volcanic crater was no less than six miles in diameter! No wonder, therefore, that Sir Archibald Geikie has described this Phlegrean episode in the evolution of what is now the Hebrides as "the most stupendous succession of volcanic phenomena in the whole geological history of Europe".

Sometimes these lava flows, which may be as much as 100 feet deep, embedded and sealed up bands of mud and peat containing pollen grains and leaves of plants which flourished at that remote period. Expert examination has brought out the surprising fact that the flora of the time was closely related to the trees and plants now found in Eastern Asia, Australia, Africa and America. Cedars and pines of Himalayan types grew on the hill slopes, as well as conifers whose nearest relatives are found nowadays in Japan. Magnolias, a genus of tree or shrub now native in the Himalayas, Japan and North America, and gingkos, a tree now native only in China, flourished in this ancient landscape; while more lowly amid the bogs grew water-lilies akin to the sacred Lotus of the Hindu.

It is thus clear that at the time when the great Hebridean chain of volcanoes was in full blast, the land surface over which the lavas were outpoured enjoyed a climate far warmer than that of the Western Islands nowadays. Astonishing as it may seem to the mind unversed in the stupendous changes revealed by the geological record, these benign conditions were shared by the whole vast volcanic province, or "Thulean Region" as it has been called—even as far north as Greenland. In that Arctic country, amid the lava flows a rich and diverse flora of Eocene date has been discovered, including sequoias, gingkos, magnolias, and more familiar trees now flourishing in our own temperate climate, such as limes, planes, oaks, poplars, walnuts, and maples. Of the animals that lived amid the tumult of the eruptions, no fossils have survived in Skye. But from what we know about the Eocene fauna elsewhere in the British Isles, we can form a clear picture of the diversity of the beasts of the field that pastured or preyed amid that weird tumultuous landscape, so many millions of years ago. The huge reptiles of former ages had now become extinct. Bulky and brainless, they had failed to survive in the struggle for existence. Mammals, many of vast size and uncouth form, but far better furnished with grey matter, were now the lords of creation.

With the abundant marine life of the period we are not here concerned, since in Eocene times the sea-coast lay far out to the west of the Hebrides.

Across the middle of what is now Skye a turbulent river flowed, which has left its water-worn pebbles, spread out upon and in turn overlaid by successive lava flows, in Glen Brittle. Conceivably this river was a large tributary of an even mightier stream, the pebble beds of which now form a conspicuous feature in the Isle of Canna; and as these contain boulders that have come from the Western Highlands, it seems clear that this river must have had its source somewhere in the mountains of Inverness-shire. We shall return to this ancient river when we come to describe the islands of Eigg and Canna.

In the second stage of their activities the chain of Hebridean volcanoes became explosive. We must picture our Skye vent as a volcano of vast proportions—probably larger and loftier than Etna today. And as happened with Etna—and indeed in Ardnamurchan, Mull and Arran—the explosive vent has shifted. At first the igneous material injected was a basic rock, which now forms the black jagged splintered masses of the Cuillins. Later the focus of intrusion moved eastward, and the material thrust upwards to form eventually a solid core in the root of the vent, was acid in character. It now forms the smoothly contoured granophyre and granite masses of the Red Hills. A basic igneous "magma", or intrusive mass, is hotter and more fluxible than an acid injection, and therefore would force the channel, as it were, for the later up-welling of acid material. The sequence from a basic to an acid magma, so clearly visible in Skye, seems to be general in plutonic activity throughout the world, and in all periods of geological history.

Since the eruptions ceased, the combined action of denudation and submergence has produced the Skye coastline we know today, with its tiered escarpments cut in the ancient lavas, and its deep indented sea-lochs, which are nothing but drowned glens. In particular, during the Glacial period the great Caledonian ice-sheet passed westward over Skye, swept away the deposits that had accumulated on the surface of the newest lavas, and left bare and gaunt the large expanses of naked, smoothed and rounded rock that are so characteristic of the island.

It is due to this complex geological structure of Skye that the scenery of the island now offers a feast of diverse grandeur—diverse alike in character, form and colour. Most of it is empty wine-dark melancholy heath, where the heather vies with the bracken and the bog-myrtle, and the almost painful silence is broken by the wailing of the muir fowl; and swart brooding peat-hags, sown with waving bog-cotton and dappled by patches of bright green grass—all sweeping up, in many an undulation or embattled breast, against the bared teeth of the Cuillins and the solemn masses of the Red Hills. But in the south-east around Sleat and Armadale, and in the north-west about Dunvegan, we find green and fertile lowlands, spangled with myriad wild flowers and varied by stout pines and graceful birches. An infinite variety of scenery marks the coastline, from the solid unindented walls of black basalt overlying streaked grey and chocolate limestones on the east side of Trotternish, through the fantastic rugged cliffs of Loch Bracadale and the emerald slopes of Loch Harport, to the gentle sands of Staffin and the shingly beaches of Broadford. Some of the cliffs are as much as 1,000 feet in height. Cavern and grotto, stack and needle, combine to form a panorama of coastal erosion unsurpassed in Britain. Over the sheer cliffs leap uncounted cascades, often tossed into wild plumes of spray by the fierce Atlantic gales.

An added witchery is lent to the landscapes of the island by the great and abrupt climatic variations to which it is subject. At one time weeping, eerie mists drift patchily across the mountains, or blot out the moorlands in a single close drenching pall of white. At another time the heavens are brilliant with meridional sunshine, and the landscape takes on varied hues in an almost Italian splendour, with the azure sea never far out of view, margined always with white foam along the winding coasts and round the rocky islets. Though the rainfall is high (about 65 inches) and the atmosphere is moist and vaporous, the climate is mild and there is little snow. Frost does not generally occur before late November. The worst climatic trials of Skye are the pitiless deluges of Atlantic rain that sometimes damage the crops in harvest time, and the sudden rainy squalls to which the inshore waters are liable.

The antiquarian and the historian vie with the geologist in their enthusiasm for Skye. Here we encounter abundant remains of the far-distant prehistoric ages—all the better preserved because cultivation has obliterated less in this wild countryside than in more favoured lands. Chambered cairns of the Stone Age, round cairns and cists of the Bronze Age, earth-houses, *duns* or dry-built forts, and brochs of the Age of Iron, all these speak to us of pagan times. The early Christian Church has left its traces in certain primitive beehive cells; in the well-preserved monastic settlements at Loch Chaluimchille in Trotternish and Annait near Dunvegan; and in the names of Celtic missionaries still clinging to little chapels which in their present form are mostly of medieval date, and contain often, in the untidy little graveyards that enclose them, beautifully sculptured cross-slabs of the period immediately preceding the Reformation. To the Middle Ages also, belong the stone-and-lime castles like Dunvegan, Duntulm and Dunscaith. Still inhabited by the same family which has held it since time immemorial, including within its rocky cincture building work of at least ten periods, and within its stately rooms containing priceless heirlooms and artistic treasures, Dunvegan Castle is beyond doubt one of the foremost of Scotland's ancient houses.

The recorded history of Skye presents every character of wild and picturesque romance. The first fair burgeoning of Celtic civilization was stamped underfoot by the fierce marauding Norsemen, who came to loot but remained to settle, and have left an enduring impression on the island's topography and racial stock. The great King Haakon Haakonsson anchored in Portree Bay on his way to disaster at Largs in 1263. In 1540 the brilliantly appointed fleet of James V, after sailing round the island and calling at Dunvegan, dropped anchor in the same harbour. Bitter conflicts between the three rival clans, Macdonalds, Macleods and Mackinnons, who struggled for mastery of the island, make up a tale full of bloodshed, yet redeemed by episodes of chivalry, fidelity and compassion.

The most recent, and certainly the most romantic chapter in the history of Skye was written in the dark days that followed Culloden, when for a week the island became the refuge of Prince Charles Edward, who owed his preservation chiefly to the dauntless resource of Flora Macdonald, Skye's most famous heroine. In modern times the island has acquired a literary glamour all its own through the visits in 1773 of Dr Samuel Johnson and James Boswell, and in 1814 of Sir Walter Scott, who has immortalized some of its finest landscapes in *The Lord of the Isles*. In a letter preserved at Dunvegan Castle Scott writes that this poem "owes its best passages to Macleod's kindness and taste in directing me to visit the extraordinary scenery between his country and Strathaird, which rivals in grandeur and desolate sublimity anything that the Highlands can produce".

The population of Skye now totals about 8,600. More than double that number of people lived in it before the middle of last century; and in the course of the Napoleonic Wars it is reckoned that the island sent over 10,000 men to serve in the British Army! During the dark years of 1914–18 more than 2,000 Skyemen, a fifth of the total population, joined up with the King's forces on land or sea or air—truly a proud and gallant record. Nor were the devotion and sacrifice of the islanders in any way diminished in the course of the Second World War; though, owing to the different conditions of that conflict, the losses suffered by the island's menfolk were happily not so great.

In recent years the rate of emigration has slowed down, thanks partly to the extensive Government schemes for the settlement of ex-Servicemen. Most of the people are engaged in crofting, sheep and cattle rearing, and to a less extent in fishing. Potatoes and oats are the chief crops. In the old droving days the island played a notable part in the cattle trade. From the Outer Hebrides the tough, shaggy little beasts were ferried over to assembly points in Skye, whence they were swum across the narrow channel of Kylerhea, landing in Glenelg, and so were driven by Spean Bridge over the Grampians to the Crieff and Falkirk Trysts. The cattle, totalling about 11,000, now belong to various West Highland breeds, and the sheep, over 100,000 in number, are mostly black-faced. The sea-fishing is mainly cod, herring, ling and salmon, with lobsters, periwinkles and oysters in certain localities.

To a very small extent, the crofters still live in the old "black houses", with their dry-built, weather-stained or lichen-splashed walls, earthen floor, and thatched roof held on by ropes weighted with large stones—sometimes even by worn-out fishing nets. In outline, these huts differ little, and in size are sometimes less than the peat stacks that adjoin them. To the sophisticated eye of the over-civilized city dweller, these abodes may look miserable enough, but they are often found to be the homes of healthy, intelligent and happy families. Rapidly, however, these primitive dwellings are being replaced by up-to-date cottages, comely and whitewashed, supplied with electricity and piped-in water. The electricity is generated at a hydro-electric station on Storr Loch.

Since the First World War, much land in Skye has been planted by the Forestry Commission, and there is a forestry school upon the island.

The islanders are mainly Celtic in race, with a strong dash of Norse blood. They are a refined and attractive people, with the innate good breeding and unstudied courtesy of the Celt. Gaelic is still their language, though unhappily it is yielding more and more to English. Those who speak Gaelic are for the most part bilingual. The great majority of the islanders belong to the Church of Scotland and the Free Church. They cherish the strict pattern of faith and conduct which marks the Presbyterian areas of the Hebrides. This attitude is most apparent in their rigid Sabbatarianism, which has caused a minority of the islanders to wage stout warfare against the proposal for a Sunday car-ferry to Kyleakin, a service that has now been introduced.

The sporting and recreational facilities offered by Skye are of a high order. On the upland moors are grouse, hare and woodcock, and the rivers and lochs are well stocked with salmon and sea and burn trout. Among the Cuillins and elsewhere the red deer is stalked. But in Skye sport, even the kingly sport of mountaineering, will always yield pride of place to sheer glory of scenery as the lodestar of the island. It is to see the varied beauties of the Misty Isle that the summer visitors throng each year in their increasing thousands. And, when we unwillingly quit its shores, the hundredfold impression of scenic delight is condensed into a sense of overpowering and haunting beauty, a beauty tinged with melancholy, which no other land can exactly give and of which no lapse of time will dim the precious memory.

Skye is upon the whole fairly well served with roads, and much is being done to improve and extend them. It is now an easy matter to visit most parts of the island by car. From Portree, the capital, roads extend northwards all round Trotternish, and across it over the Quiraing; north-westward to Skeabost and thence on to Vaternish, Dunvegan and Glendale; across the central moorland plateau to Bracadale; southward to Sligachan and thereafter along the winding coast to Broadford, from which places branches lead to Kyleakin and Elgol, and down the east side of Sleat to Armadale. From Sligachan a road leads westward to Drynoch and thence above Loch Harport to Bracadale; while from Drynoch a road runs westward to Talisker, with a branch, affording a magnificent close-up panorama of the Cuillins, conducting southward to Glen Brittle.

Skye is connected to the mainland by car-ferries between Kyle of Lochalsh and Kyleakin, between Glenelg and Kylerhea and between Mallaig and Armadale; by cargo boat between Glasgow and Armadale; and by motor vessel from Mallaig calling at Kyle of Lochalsh, Raasay and Portree. There is a bus service between Armadale, Kyleakin, Portree and Dunvegan, with through service to Uig in connection with the car-ferry to the Outer Isles. During the holiday season numerous bus tours and motor-boat cruises are available. The hotel accommodation throughout the island maintains a high standard of excellence—though, taken as a whole, the accommodation is unequal to the increasing demand. Many of the crofting townships now offer "bed and breakfast".

Dunvegan Castle, Skye

Portree

Portree, the capital of Skye, is a pleasant townlet of about 2,000 souls, snugly posted in a cup among the brown hills at the inner angle of Portree Bay, which, opening on the east side of the island at the base of Trotternish, here makes a sharp turn to the south and runs up as a shallowing and narrowing estuary into the valley of the Varragill River. On an islet in this upper part of the loch, united with the mainland at low tide, is the site of a chapel bearing the name of St Columba. The lower part of the loch forms a capacious and well-sheltered harbour, the entry to which between lofty, dark, precipitous cliffs and overhung by the great basaltic mass of Ben Tianavaig (1,352 feet) is most impressive.

The name of the town is usually derived from the Gaelic *Port-righ*, the "King's Port", and has been attributed to the visit of James V in 1540. Less romantically, the Gaelic original has been presented as *Port-righeadh*, the "port of the hill-slope".

Part of the town clusters round the pier at the base of a bold, craggy and wooded bluff known as "The Lump", crowned with a modern octagonal tower.

It may be of interest that the last hanging in Skye took place at "The Lump", on 18th June, 1742. The following paragraph appeared in the *Caledonian Mercury* of 5th July, 1742:

> Portrice [*sic*] in the Isle of Sky, June 18. The Lords of Justiciary in their last circuit at Inverness, having appointed the Sentence of Death pronounced on Angus Buchanan, convict for the Murder of James Orr, Travelling Chapman, to be put in Execution in this place, the same was accordingly done this Day with the greatest Decency and without the least Distrubance [*sic*], at sight of Alex- ander Macdonald of Kingsbrugh [Factor to Sir Alexander Macdonald, Bt.] to whom it was remitted to superintend the Execution; and the Criminal discovered a just Sense of his Guilt and Conviction. His Accomplice suffered at Inverness.

The name of the accomplice was Duncan McQueen who was hanged at the Gallowmuir, Inverness, on the same day, 18th June.

On one of the O.S. Sheets of Portree "Buchanan's Grave" is marked on "The Lump".

The remainder of the town straggles loosely up the slopes to the north and west, and encloses a spacious square, in which is the handsome war memorial, designed like an old Scottish market cross. As approached from the sea, the appearance of the white

4

4 Skye Croft in Bracadale; behind, Macleod's Tables

houses set amid the green hills is most attractive; and the town looks equally charming when seen from the neighbouring heights.

The town boasts three large hotels, the Royal Hotel, the Portree Hotel and the Coolins Hotel; several inns and ample lodging accommodation. The Royal Hotel, which fronts the bay, occupies the site of the tavern in which Prince Charles Edward took leave of Flora Macdonald, and where Johnson and Boswell called for their letters from the south. In the harbour, says Johnson, "a ship lay waiting to dispeople Skye, by carrying the natives away to America". Boswell, who went on board, noted that "the accommodation for the emigrants was very good. A long ward I may call it, with a row of beds on each side, every one of which was the same size every way, and fit to contain four people". Another thing which Boswell noted was the scarcity of ready money in Skye: "I got one and twenty shillings in silver at Portree, which was a wonderful store."

In those days the hamlet consisted merely of a few wretched thatched huts huddled together beside the harbour. Now Portree is a bright and well-appointed little town, with a secondary school, the usual profusion of churches, a library with billiard room adjoining, a nine-hole golf course, hard tennis courts, and every modern convenience. Here also are the County Buildings, housing that portion of the local administration of the island which is delegated from Inverness, to which shire Skye belongs. In the Episcopal Church, which is dedicated to St Columba, is a memorial window to Flora Macdonald.

Alongside the secondary school is the handsome and well-equipped Elgin Hostel for boys, opened by the then Duke and Duchess of York on 12th September, 1933. Nearby is the Margaret Carnegie Hostel for girls. On the summit of "The Lump" is a sunk area upon which at the end of August the Skye Highland Games are held.

A well-equipped hospital, with twelve beds of medical and maternity cases, has recently been built on a commanding site overlooking the Bay, and no more than 200 yards from the centre of the town. The hospital also contains provision for visiting consultants.

Portree has a moderately flourishing export trade, mainly in fish, cattle, sheep and wool. The only industry is a small tweed mill. The town is the centre of the road system of Skye; and as there are ample transport facilities during the season it forms an admirable base for a longer or a shorter holiday on the island. At the height of summer the bay is crowded with yachts and motor-boats, and the town then presents a bustling and picturesque appearance.

At Camas Ban, beyond Vriskaig Point, is a "pocket beach", good for bathing. Here an interesting seam of lignite was formerly worked. This represents vegetable matter, accumulated on a terrestial surface during Jurassic times, and baked into a kind of coal by igneous intrusion during the period of Eocene vulcanicity.

The immediate surroundings of Portree are full of fascinating interest. The bold cliffs, that front each other across the harbour are composed of oolite capped by thick ejections of basalt. The oolitic beds are horizontal, and consist of sandstones and shelly limestones, from which ammonites and belemnites may be collected. Belemnites are the fossil "ink-pens" of an extinct form of cuttle fish; while the great family of ammonites, coiled cephalopod shells, display such a bewildering series of varieties during the Jurassic epoch that the strata of that great system have been divided into zones according to their characteristic ammonites. At least nine of these zones have been recognized in the Jurassic beds of Skye. At Beal, near Portree, the oolitic rocks exhibit "false bedding", an irregular layering due to the fact that the sands were deposited in shallow water liable to eddies or cross currents.

These softer rocks beneath the basalt have weathered into many curious caverns and gullies. Here the botanist will join the geologist in enthusiastic exploration; for these cool shady nooks and crannies and the green slopes above them are the haunt of many rare mosses, ferns and wild flowers. The series of caves is continued along the coast to the northward; and in one of them, about five miles from Portree, Prince Charles Edward is said to have sheltered. This cave is of interest also for its stalactites and for the Liassic and Oolitic fossils to be found in it.

To the south-west of Portree is Fingal's Seat (1,367 feet). From its summit a superb view is obtained, under favourable conditions, over most of Skye, the grand mountain mass of Wester Ross, and the long line of the Outer Hebrides. The ascent of Fingal's Seat is made from the head of the golf course. It conducts us up a beautiful, narrow and rugged water channel, the lower portion of which is lined with graceful dwarf birches, while the upper part is carpeted with fern and velvet moss, and besprint with violet and primrose. At intervals in the climb, projecting knobs of lichen-stained basalt form a series of miniature and fascinating cascades.

The name "Fingal's Seat"—in Gaelic *Aite Suidhe Fhinn*—brings us immediately into contact, and upon the very threshold of Skye, with the great cycle of Ossianic poetry and legend in which the island plays so notable a part. No one now doubts that Macpherson's *Ossian*, which set Europe ablaze in the last quarter of the eighteenth century, was based to a considerable extent on original Gaelic materials, startling as were the liberties that he took in dressing these up in an English version. Equally clear is the evidence that much of his subject matter was collected in Skye—where, so Martin Martin recorded in 1695, "the natives have many stories of Finn Mac-Coul". So, in this little portrayal of the Misty Isle, we shall have much to say about Macpherson's *Ossian*; accepting it for what it is, as a work of a great poetical genius of the eighteenth century—but a work which would not have been possible but for the existence of ancient Gaelic materials.[1] In this connexion I may be allowed to quote the verdict, not of an impassioned champion of Celticism, but of a great scientist, the famous geologist, Sir Archibald Geikie. Here is what he says:-[2]

Under the stilted eighteenth century language in which Macpherson has given forth his materials, we can descry the kind of thoughts and similes for which the natural surroundings would have prepared us. Many years ago, when through each varying mood of wind and weather, Ossian and my hammer were companions in every ramble among these western moors and sea-lochs, it was strongly borne in upon my mind that, putting Macpherson aside altogether, there is in the poems of Ossian a true poetry of local form and colour, which could only have been created in the West Highlands, but which must be of old date, for it alludes to characteristics that have long passed away. The local truth of the descriptions and allusions is altogether remarkable—the golden sunsets over the western ocean, the surge of the breakers on the dark rocks of the iron-bound shore, the dimpled surface of the kyle and sea-loch as the breeze sweeps downward from the mountains, the rustle of the bent on the bare moor as the sough of the evening wind passes over it, the scattered boulders and lonely cairns, the rapid chase of sunshine and shadow as the clouds are driven over

[1] The best modern study of the Ossianic controversy is by Professor Derick S. Thomson, *The Gaelic Sources of Macpherson's "Ossian"*, 1951.
[2] *The Scenery of Scotland*, pp. 437–8.

firth and fell, the deepening gloom of the gathering storm when
the gale howls down the glens, tearing the rain-sheet into long,
swiftly following shreds, like troops of dimly seen ghosts. These
features are displayed with such simple truth that, whatever may
be the value we are disposed to set upon the poetry, we must admit
that in Scotland it could only have been born among the West
Highlands, and that it is genuine of the soil.

So upon Fingal's Seat, overlooking Portree Bay, the mighty
third-century King of Morven is said to have sat, watching the
hunting exploits in the glen below:—

"Call," said Fingal, "call my dogs, the long-bounding sons of
the chase. Call white-breasted Bran; and the surly strength of
Luath" . . . The shrill sound spreads along the wood. The sons of
heathy Cromla arise. A thousand dogs fly off at once, grey-
bounding through the heath. A deer falls by every dog; three
by the white-breasted Bran. He brought them, in their flight, to
Fingal, that the joy of the King might be great.

Trotternish

Thanks to the good road which now encircles Trotternish, the
journey round the great northern peninsula of Skye can be comfortably made by car in the course of a day, allowing ample time
to visit the numerous places of interest.

Leaving Portree by the coast, the first object of note is Dun
Gerashader, high perched on a rocky outcrop between the road
and the sea. This is one of the most interesting hill-forts on the
island. It is remarkable for its quadruple line of defence on the
only approachable side. The outer two ramparts consist of
boulders set on end. Within the enclosure are the remains of hut
circles. The fort is of large size, measuring about 168 feet in
greatest length: and the innermost or main wall, carefully built
of dry-stone masonry, has been at least 14 feet thick. Dun Gerashader is the dwelling of a fairy, who keeps three fairy cows!

Next the road passes, also on the right, two lovely lakes, Loch
Fada and Loch Leathen, and then holds nearer to the sea. Promi-
nent on the left is the mighty basaltic escarpment of Storr, its
crest topped by a succession of fantastic airy towers and pinnacles,
of which the most incredible, known as "the Old Man", is a
gigantic isolated stack, 150 feet in height, pointed above and
undercut below—in shape like a colossal fir-cone. It is a notable
landmark for sailors.

The steam or gas holes blown in the lava have in course of ages become filled with beautiful crystalline materials, forming what the geologist calls amygdaloids, from their almond-shaped forms. Some of these crystalline or sparry deposits are of great beauty, with the result that the Storr Rocks are much favoured by collectors.

One of the most remarkable instances of "treasure trove" ever recorded in Scotland took place in 1891 on the shore beneath the Old Man of Storr. The hoard consisted of 28 objects of silver, including neck rings, brooches, bracelets, and hammered ingots. Along with the bullion were recovered 110 coins, of which 92 were Anglo-Saxon silver pennies of the tenth century, and 18 were Cufic dirhems or silver coins of the Samanid Caliphs, dating from the same period, and struck at Samarkand or Esh-Shash. It seems likely that the hoard had been concealed by a Norse rover, or, less probably, by a pilgrim. The coins and bullion are now preserved in the National Museum of Antiquities of Scotland.

At Lealt, to the left of the road a little further on, diatomite is found in large quantities. This is a dry earth composed of the countless flinty cases of microscopic plants. It is used for sundry industrial purposes, including the making of dynamite. During the First World War the deposit was worked intensively, but thereafter the mine was closed. Recently it has been re-opened, though owing partly to improved processes the mine now employs no more than a handful of men.

After passing Loch Mealt on the left, the road now approaches to the very brink of the cliffs; and a view is obtained looking ahead, of the famous Kilt Rock. The upper part is vertical, composed of black columnar basalt; the lower portion consists of horizontal oolite beds, banded alternately white and grey—so that the *ensemble* gives precisely the effect of a gigantic kilt! Across the blue, wind-swept waters of the Sound is a splendid panorama of the mainland, with the high mountains that cradle Loch Carron and Loch Torridon, and midway in the narrows the brown hills of Raasay and the rugged crags of Rona.

Descending into Staffin Bay the road turns inland again and sends off to the left a branch that crosses the Storr ridge to the other side of Trotternish. This road is one of the most wildly picturesque in Skye, with its fearsome gradients and its famous hairpin bend. It affords an unrivalled view of the fantastic rocks of the Quiraing—the Needle, a single slender column, 120 feet high, and the Table Rock, a huge mass, 120 feet in length and 60 feet in breadth, standing like a billiard table of the Titans on an emerald carpet of lush grass in the middle of a great amphitheatre of black shattered cliffs. In this locality also, beautiful amygdaloidal crystals can be gathered.

It is amid this northern portion of Trotternish that the basaltic landscape of Skye makes its most powerful impact upon the imagination. Undoubtedly the chief impression is produced by the sheer savage grandeur of the rock scenery—those great grim tiered black escarpments, often columnar like Fingal's cave in Staffa; the fantastic sculpturing into spire, crocket, niche and pinnacle, for all the world like some Gothic cathedral; the unexpected caverns, ravines, and clefts. Less dramatic, but more pervasive and enduring, is the impression of melancholy left by the sterility of the landscape. Only in the broader valleys, where residual masses of boulder clay have weathered down into a subsoil reasonably fertile, will you find sizeable patches or tracts of cultivation. Elsewhere the basalt has either been scoured bare by ice, or is covered by a thick mantle of peat. Heather, coarse grasses, and lowly bog plants make up the bulk of vegetation. Cattle and sheep have long since stripped the landscape of trees: but in every little ravine or cleft up which you may force your way, and on every islet in the innumerable tarns, dwarf birch, hazel, rowan, aspen, and oak, remain to remind us that in former times Skye was a well-wooded country.

This is indeed an Ossianic landscape:

As the sudden rising of winds, or distant rolling of troubled seas, when some dark ghost in wrath heaves the billows over an isle: an isle, the seat of mist, for many dark brown years. . . . A distant sunbeam marks the hill. The dusky waves of the blast fly over the fields of grass.

Returning to the coastal road, we continue our journey round the snout of Trotternish. Nestling amid plantations betwixt the sea and the rocky and heathclad hills that rise abruptly behind, is the Flodigarry Hotel. At Flodigarry Flora Macdonald and her husband, Captain Allan Macdonald of Kingsburgh, made their home during the first twenty-two years of their married life. From the hotel terrace the view of the Ross-shire coast and hills is very grand. Beyond Flodigarry the road begins to work round

to the left, so as to get across Rhuda Hunish, the point of Trotternish, underneath the great nose of Sgurr Mor (1,460 feet)—the
terminus of the basaltic spine of the peninsula.

At Duntulm Castle, the ancient residence of the Macdonalds
of Sleat and Trotternish, the road touches the west coast. Little
now remains of the castle, of which large portions have tumbled
down in recent years. Its stance is magnificent, overhanging the
rocky and boulder strewn beach on the brink of a precipitous
mass of regularly jointed and columnar basalt, 50 feet in height.
On the landward side the castle is isolated by a deep fosse, traversed by a central earthen causeway leading to what had been
the entrance. On the east jamb of a window which had looked
out from a tower projecting into the courtyard, the plaster-work
still retains faint traces, becoming fainter every year, of the figure
of a galley incised, not unskilfully, by some idle hand. Remains
exist of a sea-gate; but how on earth this was reached from the
rocky beach far below is anybody's guess. Much of the castle
was seemingly built, or rebuilt, by Sir Donald Gorme Macdonald
of Sleat, pursuant to a directive issued in 1617 by the Privy
Council, in accordance with King James VI's vigorous and
salutary policy of disciplining the Hebridean chiefs. Sir Donald
was instructed to "make his residence and duelling at Duntillum,
and, yf he has not a sufficient comelie house ansuerable to his
estate alreddy thair, that he sall with all convenient diligence
prepair materiallis and cause build ane civil and comelie house,
and, yf his house be decayit, that he sall repair and mend the
same". The chief was further ordered to restrict his household to
six gentlemen, to limit his consumption of wine to four tuns a
year,[1] and to produce as surety for his good behaviour, three of
his principal kinsmen annually to the Privy Council!

The occupation of the castle is said to have terminated under
ghastly circumstances. A nurse accidentally dropped the infant
son of the chieftain out of a window into the sea far below. After
the tragedy the family never cared again to stay at Duntulm: but
before quitting the place—so the legend continues—the bereaved
father turned the hapless nurse adrift in an open boat full of holes.

Duntulm lies at the north end of Score Bay. At its south end
we come to the little windswept churchyard of Kilmuir. Here,
beneath a great modern Iona cross of gleaming white granite,
rests all that is mortal of Flora Macdonald, wrapped in a sheet in

[1] In the old measure, a tun of wine was 252 gallons.

which the Wanderer whom she saved slept at Kingsburgh. Nothing can be added to the immortal tribute paid to her by Johnson, who, with Boswell, were the guests of Flora and her husband at Kingsburgh on 12th and 13th September, 1773: "We were entertained with the usual hospitality by Mr Macdonald and his lady, Flora Macdonald, a name that will be mentioned in history, and if courage and fidelity be virtues, mentioned with honour. She is a woman of middle stature, soft features, gentle manners, and elegant presence."

The view from the churchyard is superb. It includes Loch Snizort, flanked by the stern cliffs of Vaternish, and far beyond it the dark blue conical hills of Harris and the long broken line of North Uist and Benbecula. In this historic churchyard is many a hoary tombstone, half obliterated by moss and lichen. By far the most notable is a slab, showing in high relief the effigy of some wild old island chief, clad in the pointed bascinet and quilted mail worn in the Hebrides during the fourteenth and fifteenth centuries. His face and neck are enveloped in a camail or chain-mail hood, like that shown on the effigy of the Black Prince in Canterbury Cathedral. He carries a great broadsword, and on either side of his head are inscribed panels in Gothic lettering. Alas! as if to mock us with the mute oblivion that has overtaken this finely wrought memorial of a great chief of other times, we can now decipher no more than the first two tantalizing words; "HIC JACET—Here lies . . ." Worn as it is, this effigy gives me the impression of a youngish man; and when I look upon it, I recall the words of Ossian: "Happy are they who fell in their youth, in the midst of their renown! They have not beheld the tombs of their friends; or failed to bend the bow of their strength."

Close beside Kilmuir churchyard a "black house" has been reconditioned and fitted up as the Skye Cottage Museum, opened in May 1965. Unfortunately the only opportunity I have had of visiting it was on a Sunday afternoon, when I found it closed, *more insulano*.

Along the coast southward from this point extends the green plain of Kilmuir. This is known as "the granary of Skye"; and its possession by the Macdonalds of Sleat was long and bitterly and bloodily contested by their inveterate rivals, the Macleods of Vaternish. In 1772, Pennant describes its fields as "laughing with corn". Midway in its broad northern portion was formerly Loch

Chaluim-chille, which was drained in 1824, but is now fast reverting to marsh. As the name suggests, the loch contained a Columban monastery, upon an island that now forms a dry stony tump rising above meadows fragrant with natural hay. The remains are still distinct, and give a good idea of a primitive Celtic monastery, with its enclosing "cashel", or dry built wall, its beehive cells, and its two small chapels. Round about are patches of stony ground, which may well cover the remains of *domunculae* or clergy-houses. This early Christian settlement would certainly repay a systematic excavation. Two dug-out canoes, one of oak and one of pine, have been found in the bed of the former loch. Doubtless they were used by the monks.

South of the monastic site a tall grey old house stands prominently forth against the skyline. This is Monkstadt (formerly Mugstot), whence Prince Charles was secretly provisioned after his landing, accompanied by Flora Macdonald, upon the beach below on 29th June, 1746. Sir Archibald Macdonald, the laird, was absent, but Flora—despite the fact that the house was occupied by a detachment of Hanoverian soldiery—succeeded in making the dangerous secret known to his wife. Meantime the Prince, disguised as her serving woman, "Betty Burke", waited on a hill near the beach. Among the house party was Macdonald of Kingsburgh, who provided himself with a bottle of wine, a glass and some biscuits, and stole forth unnoticed to find the Prince. When Kingsburgh approached, "Betty Burke" started up, and advanced in masculine posture, threatening to knock him down with a large knotted stick, till he said: "I am Macdonald of Kingsburgh come to serve your Highness."

At the south end of the Kilmuir plain the road, after receiving on the left the cross road over the Quiraing, makes a remarkable hairpin bend and descends sharply into the Bay of Uig. This is a deep, kidney-shaped indent, backed by a fine raised beach beneath a grand semicircular sweep of steep grassy braes, running out at either end into tall bluff black cliffs of basalt, and gashed midway by a couple of deep rocky gulleys, lined with birch, mountain ash and alder, and scented with ferns and wild flowers, through which the Conon and the Rha tumble noisily down to the beach. There is here a pier which serves the car-ferry from Uig to the Outer Isles. Uig is a scattered village community, with many trig cottages suitable for summer quarters, a hospital, a hotel, and a post office. The cottages have neat well-kept gardens (a thing rather unusual in Skye). The gold and emerald patchwork of the crofts, with their hay stacks, corn stacks and peat stacks, is orderly, and there is much scattered woodland. Hence the whole scene is soft and alluring—although a sterner note is sounded by the grim cliffs at either end, and the black ramparts of Vaternish across the dancing waves of Loch Snizort. Midway in the Loch are the rocky grey Ascrib Islands, a haunt of seal and lobster.

South of Uig Bay the road begins to trend inward along the east margin of Loch Snizort Beag. At the entrance to the Loch are the ruins of Caisteal Uisdein, "Hugh's Castle". All that now remains is the ground and second storeys of a large rectangular keep, with walls varying from 7 to 9 feet thick. The masonry is of early West Highland type, consisting of coursed basaltic blocks, many of which are set on end instead of being built horizontally. This masonry, coupled with the fact that the basement has not been vaulted, and the size, massive construction, and whole character of the tower, all make it certain that Caisteal Uisdein is much older than 1580, in or about which year it is traditionally asserted to have been built by Hugh Macdonald, "son of Archibald the Cleric". According to the story, Hugh built it in defiance of his uncle, the lord of Duntulm, who in retaliation seized his nephew and condemned him to a lingering death in the dungeon of Duntulm Castle. To aggravate his visitor's suffering, the ruthless chief is said to have fed him with salted beef and then left him to perish from thirst! Whatever truth may underlie this gruesome yarn, Hugh Macdonald was certainly not the builder of the castle that now bears his name. The situation of the ruined tower is splendid, on a basalt cliff rising about 45 feet sheer above the sea.

Kingsburgh House is the next place of interest. It stands amid thriving plantations, and is the modern successor of the mansion to which Flora Macdonald brought Prince Charles Edward, and which in more tranquil times entertained Dr Johnson and his biographer. Boswell's description of his host, Allan Macdonald of Kingsburgh, by then husband of Flora, is worth repeating:

He was quite the figure of a gallant Highlander—"the graceful mien and manly looks". He had his tartan plaid thrown about him, a large blue bonnet with a knot of black ribbon like a cockade, a brown short coat of a kind of duffle, a tartan vest with gold buttons and gold buttonholes, a bluish filibeg, and tartan hose. He had jet-black hair tied behind and with screwed ringlets on each side, and was a large stately man, with a steady sensible countenance.

At Snizort Church the road leaves the Loch, and at the crofting township of Borve it joins the main road from Portree by Skeabost to Dunvegan.

Skeabost and Vaternish

Skeabost, pleasantly situated at the head of Loch Snizort Beag, is a hamlet with a post and telegraph office. The River Snizort—one of the best salmon waters in Skye—is here spanned by a stone bridge. Immediately below this is a shingly islet between two branches of the stream. This islet is the site of an ancient ecclesiastical settlement, founded doubtless by St Columba, whose name it bears. There is still a little churchyard, in the usual unkempt condition of West Highland cemeteries, although it is not disused; and in the churchyard are two ruined chapels. One of these, of considerable size but now reduced to foundations, seems to be of medieval date: but the other, quite small yet in much better preservation, is of Celtic type, and its masonry is of Irish character, consisting of uncoursed polygonal blocks packed in with pinnings varying greatly in size. A few overgrown slabs show mailed effigies of the common Hebridean type, like the one we have noted at Kilmuir.

In 1922 a Viking grave was discovered at Tote, close north of Skeabost. The burial had been made within a round cairn of the Bronze Age. This cairn contained a cist, in which, however, nothing was found except a large quantity of flints. The Viking burial comprised an iron axe, portions of the wood and iron work of a shield, a bronze pennanular brooch, a bone bead, and a sandstone whetstone.

Beyond Skeabost the road hugs the west side of Loch Snizort Beag as far as the entrance to Lyndale House, at one time the seat of Lord Napier of Magdala. Here it turns westward to ascend Loch Greshornish, and a fine view of the sugar-loaf Harris mountains may be enjoyed. The little crofting township of Edinbain, with an inn, a school, and a hospital, is reached at the head of Loch Greshornish. Thence the road strikes due west across the mainland until at Fairy Bridge it meets the road which runs north from Roshill at the head of Loch Bracadale to Trumpan near the point of Vaternish.

Unlike Trotternish, Vaternish is not a peninsula of outstanding interest or beauty: though Loch Bay is a fine inlet, and the cliff scenery is imposing; while the view of swart Dunvegan Head, rising sheer to a height of 1,000 feet in the immediate forefront, with the blue Outer Isles on the horizon far beyond, is most impressive.

At Annait, a mile north of Fairy Bridge, is the site of a very early Christian settlement. The name means "mother church", and may be accepted as indicating, in all probability, that this is the most ancient ecclesiastical foundation in the district. Unhappily the name of the patron saint—who, according to Celtic practice, will have been either the actual founder of the monastery, or at all events, the founder of the parent community—has failed to reach our times. The site is a promontory between two deep basaltic gulleys; and the thick enclosing cashel wall is still well seen, with the foundations of a small chapel and sundry beehive cells. It was visited by Boswell, along with the Rev. Donald Macqueen, the learned and disputatious minister at Kilmuir, on 17th September, 1773. Macqueen introduced his companion to the "temple of Anaitis", a Syrian goddess. It is worth recalling how the penetration of Johnson, who did not accompany them, divined the true significance of these remains: "it may be a place of Christian worship, as the first Christians often chose remote and wild places to make an impression on the mind." Boswell has given us a plan of the remains—measured with his cane—and an excellent description, from which the following account of the site may be quoted:

> The place itself is green ground, being well drained by reason of a deep glen or valley on each side, in each of which there runs a rivulet or brook with a good quantity of water; for in each there are several cascades, which make a considerable appearance and sound; and at some places there are cascades formed by other brooks running into these. Upon the west there is one which has five separate falls formed by different projections of rock.

Annait of Vaternish is beyond doubt one of the most important primitive Christian sites in the Hebrides. Until the time shall come when it will be possible to carry out a systematic and careful excavation, its immunity is being jealously guarded under the provisions of the Ancient Monuments Acts.

At the village of Stein, Macleod of Macleod in the last decade of the eighteenth century planned to found a fishing station; but nothing came of the hopeful project, conceived as a means to combat the blight of emigration. Bundles of papers relating to the scheme are preserved in the muniment room at Dunvegan Castle—awaiting the time when some of our Scottish economic historians will muster up the interest and energy to examine them.

Beyond Stein the road rapidly degenerates, and ends at Trumpan. Here are the scanty ruins of an ancient church, said to have been the scene of a horrible massacre (speedily avenged from Dunvegan) of the Vaternish Macleods by their implacable enemies, the Macdonalds of South Uist. They fell on the Macleods while they were assembled for worship in the church, put fire to its thatched roof, and burned alive the whole congregation, save only for one woman, who escaped by forcing her body through a window. As the tale was told me on the spot in 1936 by a native Gael steeped in all the lore of Vaternish, she cut off a breast in order to get out. According to my informant, when the avenging Macleods arrived from Dunvegan Castle in their *birlinns*, while the fight was going on, the woman sharpened their spears, on a stone which he pointed out to me, in the burn northeast of Trumpan, above a bog myrtle bush which marks the site. The stone is a well-worn bowl with radiating blade-like marks. It is further said that the slain Macdonalds were buried by the simple expedient of ranging them in a long row at the foot of a dry-built turf dyke, and then overthrowing the dyke upon the corpses. Hence the place is still known as *Blar milléadh garaidh*—"the field of battle of the spoiling of the dyke!"

Trumpun churchyard contains some medieval grave slabs, including one displaying the effigy of a priest. Here also is a monument to the brilliant and beautiful Lady Grange. She died crazy at Trumpan in 1745, after the most heartless ill-treatment by her husband; who, afraid lest she might divulge his share in certain Jacobite plots, imprisoned her for seven long years in the remote island of St Kilda (see *infra*, p. 182).

Dunvegan Castle

Dunvegan Castle, since time immemorial the seat of Macleod of Macleod, is the most important and most renowned secular building in the Hebrides, and the only one which has been continuously occupied, and that by the same family, during a period now reaching back over a span of seven centuries. Its history, and that of the famous clan whose chiefs have ruled from their castled rock during all these many generations, is rich with drama and packed with colourful interest. In more modern times, a distinctive literary glamour has been shed round the place by the visits of Johnson and Boswell in 1773 and Scott in 1814. Within its stately halls are priceless heirlooms, some of which have descended in the hands of the Chiefs of Macleod since medieval times. The picturesqueness of the building itself is matched by its glorious surroundings. "Ane starke strengthe biggit upon ane craig", so it is described by a writer in 1549; and so it still remains. Rising sheer from the almost perpendicular edges of the rock, its massive grey walls and hoary battlements stand forth against an unrivalled background of sky and mountain and islet-spangled sea. On the landward side the Castle, no longer girt by the bare, wine-dark moorland, as when Johnson visited it, is now sheltered by extensive and thriving plantations, through which re-echoes the ceaseless murmur, and in times of spate, the loud tumult, of "Rory Mor's Nurse"—that "torrent's roaring might" celebrated by Scott in *The Lord of the Isles*. In the Dunvegan policies the luxuriance of vegetation is so extraordinary that it has been computed that at least one third of the British flora is represented in the mosses, ferns and heaths, wild and garden flowers, shrubs and forest trees. The extent of timber may be gauged from the bare fact that in the great gale of 21st March, 1921, over 40,000 trees were blown down!

Who first planted his stone fenced homestead upon the mighty basalt rock now proudly crowned by the towers and turrets of the castle, no man now can tell. But we may surely think that it was at an early date in the human settlement of Skye: for the shores of Loch Dunvegan were peculiarly suited for primitive habitation, as is shown by the numbers of ruined cairns, *duns*, brochs, and other vestiges of prehistoric dwellers which are to be seen around its green and pleasant shores. Any such traces that may still exist upon Dunvegan Rock have long since vanished from sight, buried deep beneath later buildings and the accumulated rubbish of centuries of occupation. Yet the fact of a *dun*, or early fortified settlement, is vouched for by the name itself. So we may allow ourselves to picture, in our mind's eye, the dry-built wall enclosing the turf huts huddled together on the rock, with the blue smoke curling from a hole in the thatched roof of each, or eddying forth from the low-browed doors. And our ears may catch, faintly across the centuries, the lowing of cattle, the bleat of sheep, and the cackle of poultry, all mingled with the merry cries of bairns, as they scramble about, together with the livestock, on top of the refuse heaps that cumber the space between the huts.

The castle crowns the summit of a broad, kidney-shaped basalt rock, rising about 20 feet vertically above the beach near the inner end of Loch Dunvegan, and overlooking a small natural harbour, convenient for the *birlinns* or oared galleys of those times. On the other side it is cut off by a wide rock-cut ditch spanned by a modern bridge. Boswell fancied that the Rock of Dunvegan "had been let down from heaven by the four corners, to be the residence of a chief". The oldest portion of the castle is the great ring wall or curtain, now much reduced in height. On the seaward side it retains the ancient main entrance, defended by a portcullis; thence, a steep narrow, sunk flight of steps leads up to the courtyard, passing on the right a deep well. Probably the curtain wall dates from the thirteenth century. Next in time comes the mighty keep or "great tower", of uncertain date. Its walls are 9 feet thick, and it still retains a vaulted basement and a deep, gloomy "pit" or dungeon, damp and wretched, entered originally only by a trap door from above. The Fairy Tower, with its quaint corbelled parapet, was erected by Alasdair Crottach (Crookback) early in the sixteenth century: and about 1623, the intervening range was built by the famous Sir Rory Mor. This was restored in 1686, when the fine Renaissance balustrade was added. The whole castle was remodelled twice over in the nineteenth century, and there have been important improvements, both inside and outside, in recent times.

Dunvegan Castle contains many heirlooms. Foremost is the *Bratach Sith* or Fairy Flag, a frail piece of faded and tattered silk, shot with gold thread and marked with crimson "elf-spots". It is credited with the power of thrice saving the Chief and his clan; and its efficacy is said twice to have been put successfully to the test. There is also a mazer or drinking cup of remarkable design, dated 1493. It is made of wood, mounted in silver, and was formerly richly jewelled. Rory Mor's drinking horn, a huge ox-horn banded about with silver showing delicate Celtic enrichment, supplied a formidable test of manhood for each succeeding chief, who was required to drain it empty of claret in a single draught. The horn holds nearly half a gallon! There are also a number of Jacobite relics, among them a lock of Prince Charles Edward's hair. The family portraits are of great interest, and include two Allan Ramsays and two Raeburns.

Preshal Mor above Talisker House, Skye

One of the treasures of the Castle is a remarkable sculptured stone, with Pictish symbolism, which was found at Tobar-na-Maor, near the head of Loch Dunvegan. It shows the "crescent and V-rod" and part of the "double disc and Z-rod" symbols, incised in the face of an unshapen boulder. These sculptured symbol stones are one of the great puzzles of Scottish archaeology. Their distribution is almost entirely confined to the ancient country of the Picts, to which Skye belonged until the year 670; and to that gifted people the credit for evolving so highly complex and recondite a code of symbolism must be due. The Tobar-na-Maor stone—one of three which have been recorded from the island—belongs, like the other two, to the oldest class of these monuments, in which the symbols are incised and are unaccompanied by a cross or any other recognizable mark of Christianity. Whether the symbolism was Pagan or Christian in its origin is disputed; but even the oldest class occurs again and again at known early Christian sites, and on the later monuments the symbolism in its entirety is associated, unchanged in form though elaborated in treatment, with finely carved crosses of Celtic pattern. To the meaning of the symbols, despite any amount of guessing, no key has yet been found.

A bard of Clanranald has left us a vivid picture of one of Sir Rory Mor's mighty feasts at Dunvegan, which went on for six days:

Niall Mor McVurich for Rory Mor MacLeod.

Six nights I had been in the *Dun*.
It was not a fallacious entertainment I received;
Plenty of ale was drunk at the board,
There was a large wine-hall and a numerous host.

The attendants of the house were on every side,
It was a cheerful great clan;
As quietness was better for the prince's comfort
The party of the tribe took their drink in retirement.

The merriment of the harp and of the full bowls,
With which hatred and treachery are not usually accompanied:
The laughter of the fair-haired youngsters,
We had inebriating ale and a blazing fire.

A prince from whom a good disposition is required,
He keeps the fellowship of all ecclesiastics;
In his royal court drinking is not a dream,
To his numerous company he is plentiful and hospitable.

5

The Cuillins from Sligachan, Skye

We were twenty times drunk every day
To which we had no more objection than he had;
Our mead was in abundance which consisted of
Four, three, seven along with six of varieties
Six nights.

From the northern windows of the Castle a magnificent view
is obtained down Loch Dunvegan, with its jewel-like islands like
emeralds in a silver setting, and the dark beetling basaltic brow of
Dunvegan Head beyond, while over the green and purple lower
slopes to the right the distant peaks of Harris on a clear day may
be descried. Seen from here a midsummer sunset is a sight never
to be forgotten. One such, which I watched on 13th July, 1945,
may be thus described from notes which I took down, minute by
minute. The sun set to the right of Dunvegan Head at 11.15 p.m.
(summer time):

The blazing orb sank right upon the black prow of Dunvegan
Head, disappearing finally just a little to the right of it, behind *An
Dubhaird.* I read aloud to myself Ossian's apostrophe to the Sun in
Carthon. The crimson afterglow passed up into purple banks of
cloud, flecked with touches of gold, above which appeared a clear
sky of purest liquid green and turquoise. Over this again, in the
middle height, hung an incandescent curtain of fiery mist, shading
off above into deep purple, against which puffs and wisps of cloud
stood out in darkly glowing red. All these bands of rich colour
were reflected, in reverse order, by the surface of Loch Dunvegan,
whose burnished mirror was faintly moved by a gentle western
breeze. A stately gull, like myself lost in the glory of the scene,
stood motionless upon a rock surrounded by water at the little
promontory below the billiard room window, at which I sat spell-
bound. One or two busy rabbits hopped unconcernedly about
among the grass and seaweed. In the final stage, the mist-laden sky
overhead turned to a sombre purple; while low down in the west
horizontal bars of cloud stood forth like burnished copper against
an amethystine background—sharply cut across by the bold black
outlines of Dunvegan Head and Fiadhairt. As the splendour faded,
homing gulls flew slowly in up the Loch, their plaintive cries alone
breaking the utter silence of a memorable scene.

On 31st August, 1779, when the Chief was absent on military
service in America, an attempt to raid Dunvegan Castle was made
by the famous American commodore, John Paul Jones, in his ship
the *Bonhomme Richard.* The alarm having been given by some
fishermen, Macleod's factor hastily removed all the valuables out

of the Castle. In due course the raider appeared, but was deterred from landing a party by the spectacle of a column of men, headed by pipers, marching southward along the coast towards Dunvegan. Naturally enough, Paul Jones concluded that the Fiery Cross had been sent abroad, and that the clansmen were marching in embattled array to defend their chief's stronghold. So he sheered off, and stood out from Loch Follart towards Barra. But what he had seen was nothing more than the funeral cortege of the tacksman of Swordale, on its way to the kirkyard of Kilmuir!

The neighbourhood of Dunvegan is one of the richest and most thickly settled parts of the island. At the village, about a mile south of the Castle, are two hotels, private lodging accommodation and a post and telegraph office. Dunvegan is connected by a daily bus service with Portree. The innermost recess of the Loch, with its many green islands, and embosomed in wooded hills, is one of the most charming landscapes in Skye. A conspicuous object overlooking the village is the old parish church of Kilmuir, rebuilt or repaired in 1694. In the churchyard is an obelisk erected in memory of his father, who died at Dunvegan, by Lord Lovat, of notorious "Forty-five" fame. It bears a long pompous English inscription, which Johnson scornfully suggested "Lord Lovat's butler might have written".

Of the many prehistoric monuments on either side of Loch Dunvegan the most interesting is Dun-an-Iardhard, on a peninsula about a mile north of the Castle. It is a fine example of a broch, and was carefully excavated in 1914. A miscellaneous collection of relics was found, including quantities of handmade ornate pottery, iron refuse, a necklace of fifty-nine amber beads carefully hidden in one of the wall-chambers, and bones of the ox, goat, turbary sheep and ling. The most remarkable find was a *terra-cotta* model of a bale of goods, securely packed in skins. This is of Roman origin, a votive offering to be laid by a merchant upon the altar of his patron deity, coupled with prayers for the success of his dangerous trading voyage to the Hebrides.

Along the shores of Loch Dunvegan the remains of no less than seven brochs and three *duns* have been noted. By *duns* we mean primitive fortifications consisting of one or more ramparts of loose stone, following the contours of the site, and usually enclosing hut circles. An example already noted (p. 53) is Dun Gerashader, near Portree. A broch is just a highly specialized form of *dun*. It is a circular tower of dry-built masonry, enclosing an open court. The thick wall is hollowed out with galleries, and a circular stair winds round the tower to the parapet. Round the inside there was, in some cases, a kind of penthouse, supported on posts. Many brochs have outbuildings clustered around them, usually within a defensive rampart. Three of the brochs on Loch Dunvegan illustrate this peculiarity.

Opinions upon matters of scenery will always differ: yet in my view, Loch Dunvegan is without doubt the loveliest fiord in Skye. Probably no describer of Scottish scenery was so ill to please as John MacCulloch. To his fastidious eye even the superb basalt cliffs and green terraces of northern Skye were "monotonous and tiresome". Yet he perceived the rare charm of Loch Dunvegan— or Loch Follart, to give it the older name. "I must not however pass Loch Follart," he wrote, "without pointing out the beauty of the views over its wide expanse sprinkled with islands; enhanced by the interest derived from the picturesque aspect of Dunvegan Castle." Perhaps the blue waters of the Loch, with its emerald or russet islands, fringed by golden seaweed, the swart embattled cliffs that margin its rocky shores, the green or tawny slopes with their marvellous fragrant carpet of spring and summer flowers—perhaps all these are matched elsewhere in Skye. But the singular outlines of Macleod's Tables (p. 69) like a pair of sinister couchant monsters, the far-off conical spires of Harris, the glittering white coral sands below Claigan, and the dark umbrageous, sweetly-scented woods that embosom the hoary castle—these are the things that give Loch Dunvegan a character of its own.

On the shores of Loch Bay, an alcove north of Dunvegan, we find one of the most interesting geological localities in Northern Skye. Here an outcrop of the Jurassic rocks is preserved, sealed up beneath the basaltic lavas, and now exposed by the incutting of the sea. These rocks consist of limestones and sandstones, and contain many fossil shells and some scanty remains of fishes. Formed originally as muds and sands in shallow waters, they were later consolidated and upheaved, to become, after aeons of time, the land surface over which the Eocene lavas were outpoured.

Duirinish

On the western side of Loch Dunvegan is the broad peninsula of Duirinish, with Macleod's Tables in its midst, and Ben Idrigill

(1,117 feet) at its southern end, which runs out into the great black headland of Idrigill Point, the northern sentinel of Loch Bracadale. Just outside the Point are Macleod's Maidens, three lofty slender basalt stacks. The tallest is nearly 150 feet in height and contains ten successive sheets of basalt. Macleod's Maidens are said to be a haunt of mermaids. On the south coast of Duirinish we meet with what is perhaps the grandest cliff scenery in Skye. The coast consists of perpendicular walls of basalt, here and there whitened with brine, and eroded into many a gulley, chasm and cavern, amid which the thunder of the crowding billows is tenfold magnified. The mansion of Orbost, finely situated on a terrace backed by moorland and overlooking a sandy cove which forms an inner arm of Loch Bracadale, is a good point from which to visit Macleod's Maidens.

Macleod's Tables, which dominate the views throughout north-western Skye, are two immense flat-topped horizontal cakes of basalt, reaching a height respectively of 1,538 feet and 1,601 feet. In Gaelic they are termed Healaval Mor and Healaval Beg. On Healaval Mor, the lower but broader of the two, Alasdair Crottach is said to have entertained King James V in 1536 to the famous open-air banquet, where the family candlesticks of which he had boasted to the King at Holyrood appeared as a circle of his kilted clansmen, each holding aloft a flaming torch. The story was adapted by Sir Walter Scott to provide one of the most effective scenes in *A Legend of Montrose*.

Among the lava flows of Macleod's Tables are embedded remains of Eocene land surfaces, formed during intervals of quiescence amid the volcanic outbursts. From these fossil soils well preserved leaves of forest trees have been collected.

The northern portion of Duirinish contains the pleasant valley of Glendale, where modestly thriving crofting townships flourish. In crofting history Glendale is famous, for here in 1882 took place the famous riot that led to the appointment of a Royal Commission next year and to the passing of the first Crofters' Holding Act in 1886.

Near the mouth of Loch Dunvegan is the clachan of Borreraig, where of old dwelt the remarkable family of the Macrimmons, for generations hereditary pipers to Macleod of Dunvegan. Dunvegan Head, the northmost point of Duirinish, has been more than once mentioned already. It is a superb basalt promontory, 1,000 feet in height. Engulfed in the basalt is a seam of pure coal, about a foot thick. This represents a layer of vegetation which was overrun and carbonized by the molten lava.

Loch Bracadale

The road from Vaternish and Dunvegan continues along the braes above Loch Bracadale and Loch Harport to Drynoch at the head of the latter, and thence strikes across the waist of Skye up Glen Drynoch to Sligachan. The views of mingled loch and mountain scenery obtained by this route are among the most varied and entrancing in Skye, and are held by not a few to justify their claim that Loch Bracadale, rather than Loch Dunvegan, is the loveliest fiord in the island.

As we approach Drynoch, the grandly serrated ridge of the Cuillins grows ever more dominant and impressive; while across the countless laughter of the sun-kissed waves in Loch Bracadale the low green lift of Canna, the upstanding multiple mountain mass of Rum, and the sharp nose of Eigg come successively into view. Far out in the horizon, in clear weather, the vague hills of South Uist and Barra may be seen. Above Vatten, on the right of the road, are two conspicuous round cairns, probably dating from the Bronze Age. Talisker Point, a black basalt wall 900 feet in height, now comes into view ahead. After passing on the right Ulinish House, where Boswell, greatly to his surprise, found "a plentiful garden and several trees", the road turns inland up the side of Loch Beag to Struan and the disused barn-like church of Bracadale. At Struan are a hotel and a post office.

Overlooking the road are Dun Mor and Dun Beag. The latter is the finest broch in Skye. Its wall, about 12 feet thick and beautifully fitted together of regularly coursed basalt blocks, survives to a height of about 12 feet. This broch was visited by Johnson and Boswell with Mr Macqueen, on the morning of 22nd September, 1773.

In noting the view from Dun Beag, Boswell gives his only descriptive note on the Cuillins. Like all travellers of his time, he held mountains in abhorrence. Here is what he has to say: "From this old tower, or *dun*, or whatever it shall be called, is a grand view of the mouth of Loch Bracadale, and, at a distance, Barra and South Uist; and on the land side, the Cuillin, a prodigious range of mountains, capped with rocks like pinnacles in a strange variety of shapes." He was sufficiently impressed to sketch a profile of the mountain range, which unfortunately has not survived among his papers. By the afternoon, he informs us, the Cuillins had received their first whitening with snow.

In 1915 Dun Beag was excavated. A large number of objects in stone, bronze, lead, gold, iron, glass, bone, horn and pottery were found. A bronze buckle and gold ring of Norse type pointed to a call by Viking raiders; while coins ranging from Henry II to George II must have been dropped by casual visitors, such as Johnson and his companions. An interesting discovery, dating, it would seem, from the primary occupation, was a cake of oat or rye seed.

On the opposite side of Loch Harport, and near its head, is the famous Talisker Distillery. The water which serves it descends over thirteen cascades; and a pleasantly distinctive flavour is given to the whisky by the peat used to dry the grain. Hard by is Cuchullin's Well, which Boswell tasted, and found the water "admirable". He tells us that the well is "said to have been the favourite spring of that ancient hero"—yet another proof of the part played by Skye in the Ossianic traditions. On the shore hereabouts Boswell noted the amygdaloidal infilling of the gas vesicles in the basalt.

From Carbost, a hill track leads across to the head of Loch Eynort. The River Drynoch, which the road now hugs on its way to Sligachan, affords good salmon fishing. From Drynoch, at its mouth, a branch road leads southward to Glen Brittle, where there is a youth hostel, and Glenbrittle House, suitable as headquarters for the southern Cuillins. Looking out between the lofty headlands that clasp Loch Brittle, an imposing view is obtained of Rum. From Glen Brittle an unrivalled comprehensive view of the whole vast craggy mass of the Cuillins can be enjoyed. It provides a mountain profile without parallel in Britain. A raised beach forms the floor of the glen; its slopes are walls of basalt, while high over all on the eastern side tower the awe-inspiring peaks of splintered gabbro. Glen Eynort and Glen Brittle have both profited greatly, in their upper levels, through the plantations of the Forestry Commission.

At Borline on the west side of Loch Eynort, near its head, is the ruined church of Kilmoruy, St Maelrubha's Church. No doubt this very ancient ecclesiastical centre was a foundation of St Maelrubha in person, or by a mission sent out from his famous monastery at Applecross in Wester Ross. St Maelrubha, who came from Bangor in Ulster to Applecross in 673, is one of the greatest and

most attractive figures in the early religious history of Scotland.
He died, aged eighty, at Applecross on 21st April, 722:

> In Alba[1] in shining purity
> Having relinquished all happiness
> Went from us to his mother
> Our brother Maelrubha.

The long continued sanctity of his foundation at Borline is
indicated by the shaft, still standing in the churchyard, of a noble
Celtic High Cross, belonging to the distinctive Hebridean type of
the later Middle Ages. In front it displays the Crucifixion, below
which is the figure of an abbot, fully vested. Doubtless this is
intended as a portrait of St Maelrubha. On the reverse side of the
cross-shaft is a foliaceous and zoomorphic pattern. Other late
medieval grave-slabs in the churchyard attest the importance of
this burying ground, which undoubtedly has been one of the
chief holy places in Skye. Further proof, not only of the sanctity
of the church but of its wealth, is to be found in the font, now
preserved in the National Museum of Antiquities at Edinburgh.
It displays, in bold relief, portrayals of the Crucifixion, St Michael,
the Virgin and Child, and a mitred abbot or bishop. The font
bears the date 1430.

Sligachan and the Cuillins

If Portree is the most convenient centre for the visitor who
wishes to obtain a general acquaintance with Skye, the mountaineer on the other hand will infallibly settle at Sligachan. It is
9½ miles south of Portree, and is reached by the main road
ascending Glen Varragill; or, from the opposite side, along the
winding coastal road from Kyleakin via Broadford, round the
head of Loch Ainort, and then across to the south side of Loch
Sligachan. Coming from Portree, as one nears Sligachan, the
Red Cuillins on the left, and the Black Cuillins on the right,
become every moment more awe-inspiring in their contrasted
outlines. The Black Cuillins, carved out of gabbro, exhibit their
shattered and splintered pinnacles, sharp ridges and precipitous
crags; while the granophyre Red Cuillins have weathered into
smoothly contoured, dome-like masses. Nowhere else in Britain

[1] The ancient name of Pictland. The quotation is from the *Martyrology of
Oengus*.

will you find a more impressive demonstration of the grand way in which scenery is moulded by geology.

The Sligachan Hotel is specially equipped for mountaineers; and there is good sea-trout fishing during the season in the River Sligachan. There is a post and telegraph office in connexion with the hotel.

Glen Sligachan, as seen from the hotel, is an excellent example of a U-shaped glacial valley. The basin in which stands the hotel is cumbered with morainic detritus. The great valley, scoured out by a glacier long ago, is out of all proportion to the slender stream that now descends it. In its middle portion, the course of the river corresponds almost exactly with the boundary between the gabbro of the Cuillins and granophyre of the Red Hills.

Sligachan is said to mean "the place of the shell". I do not presume to guess whether this designation was applied to it by reason of the vast basin in which the famous mountain resort now stands. But, having regard to the good cheer for which the place is now renowned, it is a tempting fancy now to invest the name with an Ossianic *aura*; for were not Fingal's heroes accustomed to drink their wine out of scallop shells, sometimes studded with gems? This we may learn from many passages in Macpherson's poems. "Often did they feast in the hall, and send round the joy of the shell." Fingal himself is described as "the King of generous shells". "Bring hither, Oscar, the deer!" he commands. "Prepare the feast of the shells. Let our souls rejoice after danger, and our friends delight in our presence!"

I have no acquaintance with mountaineering in the Cuillins, nor lies it within the compass of the present work to proffer guidance to the devotees of this austere and arduous calling. Climbers who wish practical information are therefore referred to the admirable *vade mecum* published by the Scottish Mountaineering Association. Aesthetic evaluations of these peerless summits, in all their changeful moods of mildness and wrath, will be found in the eloquent writings of Alexander Smith, J. A. MacCulloch and Seton Gordon.

The hidden beryl of the Cuillins, which no visitor to Skye will wish to leave unseen, is, of course, dark Loch Coruisk. It may be reached from Sligachan by an arduous 9-mile tramp and climb over the rocky ridge of Druim Hain, or more easily by sea from Loch Scavaig; or from Strathaird by Camasunary and the treacherous "Bad Step" beneath Sgurr-na-Strigh. Loch Coruisk has been the theme of so many descriptive rhapsodies that I shall forbear to add to their number. I content myself with referring the gentle reader to the most famous of all, that which Sir Walter Scott has given us in *The Lord of the Isles*. Scott makes his hero, Bruce, approach the Loch from the sea, as the poet himself had done when he visited it in 1814; and in his *Journal* he has left us a description of the Loch in prose which is surpassed only by his own verse. It was the Wizard of the North's description of

> that dread lake
> With its dark ledge of barren stone.

that first discovered to the English-speaking world the grandeur and the sublimity of Skye:

> Such are the scenes, where savage grandeur wakes
> An awful thrill that softens into sighs;
> Such feelings rouse them by dim Rannoch's lakes,
> In dark Glencoe such gloomy raptures rise:
> Or farther, where, beneath the northern skies,
> Chides wild Loch Eribol his caverns hoar—
> But, be the minstrel judge, they yield the prize
> Of desert dignity to that dread shore,
> That sees grim Coolin rise, and hears Coriskin roar.

Loch Coruisk is a typical glacial lake, scooped out of the gabbro by the enormous weight and slow movement of an ice stream. Its maximum ascertained depth is 125 feet; its bottom is thus 100 feet below sea level. The bare rock surfaces around are smoothed and heavily striated, or scored, by boulders carried with the glacier.

Broadford and Strathaird

For the eastern summits of the Cuillins proper, and for the Red Hills, a convenient headquarters is Broadford, which is also the best centre for visiting Strathaird and Sleat. Broadford is a sheltered, pleasant village, lying on the western arc of a raised beach above a wide semicircular shingly bay, backed by green slopes lifting into heath, and dominated by the great pink granophyre conical mass of Beinn-na-Cailleach (2,403 feet). As seen from Broadford, the smoothly contoured outline of its north-eastern flank is broken, near the summit, by a sharp dark ridge, formed by a mass of older basaltic rocks, 50 feet wide, faulted down amid the granophyre. Bold atop and scree-strewn on the flanks, this noble mountain is crowned by a cairn beneath which, so says tradition, a Norse princess sleeps. The Gaelic name signifies the Ben of the Old Woman: but this may refer not to the Norse princess, but to the Cailleach Bheurr, the colossal old deer-goddess of pagan Celtic mythology, who could wade across the deepest fiord, and whose bath-tub was the mighty whirlpool of Corrievreckan, between Jura and Scarba.

At Broadford are a pier, a post office, a bank, and two hotels, while a number of the neat white cottages cater for summer visitors. The village has a new hospital, with 24 beds, a maternity unit, and a resident surgeon. On the west side of the main road, just south of the pier, are the remains of a chambered cairn, in which were found an urn, a flint arrow-head, and a stone bracer, or archer's wrist-guard.

Broadford Bay is of much geological interest. Most of the village and the surrounding crofts stand on an ancient raised beach. In the rock exposures of the foreshore Liassic fossils are abundant, the most characteristic being the graceful bivalve Lamellibranch shell, *Gryphaea arcuata*. It occurs in great profusion, and generally well preserved. The Jurassic rocks are much disturbed by Eocene dykes, mostly of hard basalt, which stand up as rocky ridges on the foreshore. Some of these dykes have been broken across, and the disrupted sections shifted apart, by subsequent earth movements. Others include in their mass chunks, partly "digested", of the rocks into which they were injected. The trend of these intrusions is south-eastward from the great volcanic complex of the Cuillins. In the neighbourhood of Broadford the geologist will find an interesting group of sills, as well as these dykes. A sill is a horizontal injection of molten matter among older rocks, whereas a dyke (as its name implies) is more or less vertical. Some of the sills in the Broadford group are composite. The first injection was of basalt. This was later followed by felsite, which forced the basalt asunder, and along the surfaces of junction greatly altered its chemical and lithological character. Altogether, Broadford is geologically one of the most interesting areas in the Hebrides.

The whole wide curve of the bay is thickly scattered with crofts, from whose reeking "lums" a pleasant odour of peat is diffused. In front lies the low grassy island of Pabbay, and beyond it loom the dark stern mountains of Wester Ross. The sea fishing in the bay is excellent.

The little island of Pabbay, which can be reached at any time, when the weather permits, by boat from Broadford, is not without interest. It is entirely composed of Jurassic (lower Lias) strata, rich in fossils. The name is derived from the Norse word *papa*, priest, and indicates that when the pagan Vikings landed here they found a Christian settlement. Within a derelict graveyard on the side of a tiny stream may still be seen the foundations of a small stone-and-lime chapel. Adjoining turf foundations may represent the clergy-houses. Four hundred years ago the little island was well wooded.

In 1844 the fossiliferous strata of Pabbay aroused the unbounded enthusiasm of Hugh Miller:

> He would be a happy geologist who, with a few thousands to spare, could call Pabba his own. It contains less than a square mile of surface; and a walk of little more than three miles and half along the line where the waves break at high water brings the traveller back to his starting point; and yet, though thus limited in area, the petrifactions of its shore might of themselves fill a museum. They rise by thousands and tens of thousands on the exposed planes of its sea-washed strata, standing out in bold relief, like sculpturings on ancient tombstones, at once mummies and monuments—the dead and the carved memorials of the dead. Every rock is a tablet of hieroglyphics, with an ascertained alphabet; every rolled pebble a casket, with old pictorial records locked up within.

From Broadford a road leads through the lovely Strath Suardal across the narrow neck to the head of Loch Slapin, and thence is continued down to Elgol near the point of Strathaird. In a typical Skye mist this valley can be quite eerie, and indeed it is haunted by a goblin, Ludag. Of this fearsome being Hugh Miller has given us a blood-curdling description. "The waste is haunted, say the Highlanders, by Ludag, a malignant goblin, that in the last age [the eighteenth century] used to be seen at dusk hopping with immense hops on its one leg—for unlike every other denizen of the supernatural world, it is not furnished with two—and that, enveloped in rags, and with fierce misery in its hollow eye, has dealt heavy blows, it is said, on the cheeks of benighted travellers."

Shortly after leaving Broadford, the ruined farm-house of Coirechatachan is seen on the right, at the base of Beinn-na-Cailleach. It was here that Johnson behaved himself "like a buck indeed", taking a married lady of the household on his knee, and allowing himself to be kissed by her. On another evening Boswell overdid his acquaintance with his host's capacious punch bowl, got to bed fuddled at five a.m., and woke up next day (a Sunday) at noon "with a severe headache"—and yet more severe self-reproaches. "When I rose, I went into Dr Johnson's room, and taking up Mrs Mackinnon's prayer book, I opened it at the twentieth Sunday after Trinity, in the epistle for which I read, 'And be not drunk with wine, wherein there is excess.' Some would have taken this as a divine interposition."

Further on is the desolate Loch Cill Christ, and at its lower end Kilchrist, the ruined parish church of Strath. Along the road here are outcrops of a fine white marble, a metamorphic rock formed by the action of igneous injections upon the local Cambrian limestone. Beautiful, richly-carved slabs of it may be admired in some of the fireplaces at Armadale Castle. One is glad to say that this rock is now once again being quarried.

North-west of Kilchrist, along the southern flank of the much later intruded granophyre mass of Beinn-na-Cailleach, is the vent of one of the explosive centres in the earliest phase of the vast complex Eocene volcano of Skye. The crater, partly encroached upon by the granitic mass, measured no less than 3 miles across. After the explosions the vent was left choked with an agglomerate of fragments (mostly Torridonian sandstone and basalt), blown from the surrounding rocks. Later, this loosely adherent mass was invaded from below by an injection of granitic material, so as to form a rim or margin of the acid rock all round the inside of the vent. The geologist who is on the alert for evidences of the way in which scenery is conditioned by rock structure will note with interest, in this remarkable exposure, the contrasts between the low escarpments of the Cambrian limestone, the confused knobby appearance of the agglomerate, and the smooth contours of the granite.

At the crofting township of Torrin (near which are some galleried *duns*) the road comes down on Loch Slapin and thereafter circles round its head, mounting the shoulder of An Carnach and affording a magnificent view of Blaven's sinister, splintered front. Along the eastern side of Strathaird the soil is fertile and carries a considerable, though scattered population. But then the road enters more barren country, and, sweeping across the flank of Ben Meabost, crosses over to the other side of the narrowing peninsula and descends steeply to its terminus at Elgol, on the shore of Loch Scavaig. It was from here that Prince Charles, on the evening of 4th July, 1746, was rowed across to the mainland, quitting forever the shores of Skye that had sheltered him so staunchly and so surely. The cave where he lay in concealment is about a mile south of Elgol village. From here a splendid panorama of the Cuillins is obtained, seen across the dark waters of Loch Scavaig. Out in front is the island of Soay; and beyond Soay to the left a fine group is formed by the three islands of Eigg, Rum and Canna.

The glory of Strathaird is the celebrated Spar Cave, which lies on the east side of the peninsula about a mile or so from its point. The cave is best reached from the township of Glasnakille, where a boat may be hired if the sea is quiet. This is the

> mermaid's alabaster grot
> Who bathes her limbs in sunless well
> Deep in Strathaird's enchanted cell.

of which the hapless page Allan, in *The Lord of the Isles*, is dreaming at the moment when he is stabbed to death by the ruffian Cormac Doil. I cannot do better than subjoin the brilliant picture which Sir Walter Scott has given us in his *Journal*: premising only, that the depredations wrought by visitors which he castigated have, in the century and half that have elapsed since he visited the cave done much still further to abate its virgin beauty:

The first entrance to this celebrated cave is rude and unpromising; but the light of the torches with which we were provided was soon reflected from the roof, floor and walls, which seem as if they were sheeted with marble, partly smooth, partly rough with frostwork and rustic ornaments, and partly seeming to be wrought into statuary. The floor forms a steep and difficult ascent, and might be fancifully compared to a sheet of water, which, while it rushed whitening and foaming down · a declivity, had been suddenly arrested and consolidated by the spell of an enchanter. Upon attaining the summit of this ascent, the cave opens into a splendid gallery, adorned with the most dazzling crystallisations, and finally descends with rapidity to the brink of a pool, of the most limpid water, about four or five yards broad. There opens beyond this pool a portal arch, formed by two columns of white spar, with beautiful chasing upon the sides, which promises a continuation of the cave. One of our sailors swam across, for there is no other mode of passing, and informed us (as indeed we partly saw by the light he carried) that the enchantment of Macalister's cave terminates with this portal, a little beyond which there was only a rude cavern, speedily choked with stones and earth. But the pool, on the brink of which we stood, surrounded by the most fanciful mouldings, in a substance resembling white marble, and distinguished by the depth and purity of its waters, might have been the bathing grotto of a naiad. The groups of combined figures projecting, or embossed, by which the pool is surrounded, are exquisitely elegant and fanciful. A statuary might catch beautiful hints from the singular and romantic disposition of these stalactites. There is scarce a form or group on which active fancy may not trace figures or grotesque ornaments, which have been gradually moulded in this cavern by the dropping of calcareous water hardening into petrifications. Many of those fine groups have been injured by the senseless rage of appropriation of recent tourists; and the grotto has lost (I am informed) through the smoke of torches, something of that vivid silver that was originally one of its chief distinctions. But enough of beauty remains to compensate for all that may be lost.

Kyleakin, Sleat and Armadale

The road leading out of Broadford eastward forks at the further end of the bay. The left branch stops at Kyleakin. The right branch continues down the peninsula of Sleat to Aird, beyond Armadale Castle; thence a rough track goes as far as Aird Point or Point of Sleat. From Lusa Bridge, midway between Broadford and Kyleakin, a steep mountain road leads up Glen Arroch and over to the car-ferry at Kylerhea.

Kyleakin—for many the point of entry into Skye, since between it and Kyle of Lochalsh on the mainland a car-ferry constantly plies—is a pleasant village, with a post office and three hotels, as well as several boarding houses. It is dominated from the south by a green knoll crowned by the shattered ruins of a gaunt tower, Castle Maol, anciently known as Dun-na-kyne, and for centuries a seat of the Mackinnons. The walls are 9 feet thick, and the masonry is banded rubble of an early type. This fact, coupled with the lack of vaulting, suggests that the tower could be as old as the thirteenth or fourteenth century. The joints between the stones have been freely "buttered over" with coral lime.

West of Kyleakin the long low coastline shows a fine example of a raised beach. The rock here, continued southward as the backbone of Sleat, is Torridonian sandstone. This remarkable formation, classic in the history of geological investigation in

the Western Highlands and Islands, consists of unaltered sandstones, overlying the gneiss, yet older than the Cambrian. From
the Cambrian rocks they are sundered by an enormous uncon-
formity, which shows that an incalculable period of denudation
must have intervened between the laying down of the Torridon
sandstones and the deposition on their wasted surfaces of the
Cambrian limestones, shales and quartzites. Not only this, but the
Torridonian rocks in Sleat have an ascertained thickness of at
least 12,000 feet, and this must represent an unimaginable period
of deposition. To us creatures of a fleeting three score years and
ten, the geological time-scale is no less incomprehensible than the
vistas opened into unfathomable space by the modern astronomer
and physicist.

In the sheltered waters of Kyleakin King Haakon's proud
armada anchored awhile on its way southward to Largs. Kyleakin makes quite a convenient centre for visiting the Cuillins.

If the plain of Kilmuir is the granary of Skye, the eastern coast
of Sleat is unquestionably its garden. Nowhere else in the island
is the vegetation so lush, the flowers so varied and so brilliant and
so fragrant, the parkland so green, the woods so deep and spacious.
A continuous string of crofts and crofting townships, interspersed
with larger farmsteads, extends the whole length of this favoured
coast. Across the Sound of Sleat a series of ever-changing views
is enjoyed of the Kintail and Knoydart mountains. Approaching
Isle Ornsay (St Oran's island) the road passes Duisdale Hotel,
surrounded by pleasant gardens and woodland policies. At Isle
Ornsay are a pier, a post office, and a hotel.

The tottering fragment of Castle Camus, or Knock Castle, and
the ruined church of Kilmore, bearing the date 1687, are successively passed. Knock Castle is haunted by a *glaistig*, or female
sprite, who can be propitiated by libations of milk. Our road now
skirts the extensive woods and highly embellished policies of
Armadale Castle, a modern edifice, built in 1815–19. In its
predecessor (on a different site), Johnson and Boswell were in-
adequately entertained by Sir Alexander Macdonald, whose
people, in Johnson's caustic phrase, "blessed his back". The present
mansion (unhappily no longer occupied) is the seat of Lord
Macdonald. Externally and within, the castle, built in a sort of
Tudor style, is a magnificent structure. The architect was Gillespie
Graham, but a large addition was made by David Bryce. The
ample demesne in which it stands (though now, like the castle,

Loch Coruisk from Sgurr na Stri, Skye
Broadford and the Red Hills, Skye

much neglected), with its broad verdant lawns, thick hedgerows, and the umbrageous scented woodlands, containing many exotic trees and shrubs, suggest England rather than the Hebrides. In the hall of the castle is an imaginary portrait, in stained glass, of Somerled, the ancestor of the Lords of the Isles. He is depicted as a stern-looking warrior in chain mail. From the castle terrace there is a superb view across to Arisaig, Morar, Knoydart and Glenelg.[1]

At Armadale Pier, south of the Castle, the ferries from Mallaig call daily (except Sundays) during the season. At Ardvasar, about a mile to the south, are a hotel and a post office. Beyond Ardvasar the fertile country soon ceases, and the Point of Sleat is a wild and barren tangle of gneiss ribs and bosses and boulders, dark heath, and sour tarns. At the crofting and fishing township of Aird all pretence of a road ceases; but a track leads to the Point of Sleat, the most southerly headland of Skye.

Midway on the west side of Sleat is Dunscaith Castle, the most remote and by far the most interesting baronial ruin in Skye. It is reached by a branch road which, leaving the highway about 3 miles south of Isle Ornsay, crosses the Torridonian midrib of the peninsula to Ord on Loch Eishort, and returns by the township of Tarskavaig and Achnacloich to the main road above Armadale. From this road some of the finest views in Skye may be enjoyed.

Dunscaith Castle stands on a rock about 40 feet high, overlooking Loch Eishort, and isolated from the mainland by a chasm 20 feet wide. This was spanned by a drawbridge contained within a barbican, the side walls of which are carried upon two arches spanning the gulley. From the inner portal of the barbican a flight of steps mounts to the main gate of the castle. In the north-east corner of the courtyard is the prison; on the far point of the promontory remain the foundations of the hall, and in the centre of the enclosure is the well. The buildings had been of considerable extent, but are now greatly ruined and fast disappearing.

According to old Celtic legend this was the residence of Scathac the Wise, Queen of Skye, from whom the castle takes its name. Hither came the hero Cuchullin, and from the wise queen's lips learned the high arts of peace and war. Here also in after times his lovely wife, the high-bosomed Bragéla, awaited in vain her lord's return from the cruel wars west-overseas. No historic site in all Scotland is more invested in the rainbow mist of Ossianic legend:

[1] A proposal is now afoot to convert Armadale Castle into a hotel.

Dunscaith Castle
Dun Telve Broch, Glenelg

O strike the harp in the praise of my love, the lonely sunbeam of Dunscaith. Strike the harp in the praise of Bragéla, she that I left in the Isle of Mist, the spouse of Semo's son! Dost thou raise thy fair face from the rock to find the sails of Cuchullin? The sea is rolling distant far; its white foam deceives thee for my sails. Retire, for it is night, my love; the dark winds sing in thy hair.

Spread now thy white sails for the Isle of Mist. See Bragéla leaning on her rock. Her tender eye is in tears; the winds lift her long hair from her heaving breast. She listens to the breeze of night, to hear the voice of thy rowers, to hear the song of the sea! The sound of thy distant harp!

It is the white wave of the rocks, and not Cuchullin's sails. Often do the mists deceive me, for the ship of my love! when they rise round some ghost, and spread their grey skirts on the wind. Why dost thou delay thy coming, son of the generous Semo? Four times has autumn returned with its winds, and raised the seas of Togorma, since thou hast been in the roar of battles, and Bragéla distant far! Hills of the Isle of Mist! when will ye answer to his hounds? But ye are dark in your clouds. Sad Bragéla calls in vain! Night comes rolling down. The face of ocean fails. The heath-cock's head is beneath its wing. The hind sleeps, with the hart of the desert. They shall rise with the morning's light, and feed by the mossy stream. But my tears return with the sun. My sighs come on with the night. When wilt thou come in thine arms, O chief of Erin's wars?

Glenelg: the Ancient Gateway of Skye

We have mentioned (see p. 79) the car-ferry to Kylerhea. In days before motor transport, and before the opening in 1898 of the railway to Kyle of Lochalsh, the Kylerhea crossing, reached down Glenelg, was emphatically the chief communication between the Scottish mainland and Skye. By it Johnson and Boswell approached the island in 1773: though, instead of crossing direct, they were boated down the Sound of Sleat to their stingy host at Armadale. By the Kylerhea crossing, in reverse, enormous droves of cattle were swum across from Skye, and through Skye from the Outer Isles, en route for the Crieff or Falkland Trysts. It was thus in very truth the old-time gateway of Skye. Not only this, but in 1292 Glenelg was included in the Sheriffdom of Skye; while from 1343 until 1811 it belonged to the Macleods of Dunvegan. Always, therefore, its history has been intimately associated with that of the Isle of Mist; and having come down upon Kylerhea, it is thus incumbent upon us to make the narrow crossing—only about a furlong, yet often swept by fierce tidal races—and briefly to glance at Glenelg. We shall find it a district of rewarding interest.

Hugh Miller, who sailed in the *Betsey* through Kylerhea in 1844, has left us a vivid account of his experience:

Never, except perhaps in a Highland river big in flood, have I seen such a tide. It danced and wheeled, and came boiling in huge masses from the bottom; and now our bows heaved abruptly round in one direction, and now they jerked as suddenly round in another; and though there blew a moderate breeze at the time, the helm failed to keep the sails steadily full. But whether our sheets bellied out, or flopped right in the wind's eye, on we swept in the tideway, like a cork caught during a thunder shower in one of the rapids of the High Street.

A writer of 1813 has given us the following shocking picture of how the poor cattle were swum across from Kylerhea to Glenelg:

All the cattle reared in the Isle of Skye which are sent to the Southern markets pass from the Island to the mainland by the ferry of Caol Rea. Their numbers are very considerable, by some supposed to be 5,000 but by others 8,000 annually, and the method of ferrying them is not in boats as is done from the Long Island where the passage is broad, but they are forced to swim over Caol Rea. For this purpose the drovers purchase ropes which are cut at the length of 3 feet, having a noose at one end. This noose is put round the under jaw of every cow, taking care to have the tongue free. The reason given for leaving the tongue loose is that the animal may be able to keep the salt water from going down its throat in such a quantity as to fill all the cavities in the body, which would prevent the action of the lungs: for every beast is found dead and said to be drowned at the landing place to which this mark of attention has not been paid. Whenever the noose is put under the jaw, all the beasts destined to be ferried together are led by the ferryman into the water until they are afloat, which puts an end to their resistance. Then every cow is tied to the tail of the cow before until a string of 6 to 8 be joined. A man in the stern of the boat holds the rope of the foremost cow. The rowers then ply their oars immediately. During the time of high water or soon before or after full tide is the most favourable passage because the current is then least violent. The ferrymen are so dexterous that very few beasts are lost.

The hazards of crossing between Kylerhea and Glenelg are to some extent lessened by the fact that, when the tide is in race, there is an inshore eddy on whichever side is opposite to the tidal flow. Of this advantage the ferrymen today, as doubtless were the cattle drovers of old, are well able to take full advantage. The last drove is believed to have crossed Kylerhea about 1906.

Probably Glenelg is the only place-name in Britain which reads the same both ways. What the second half of the name signifies I do not know. Roomy and airy, and enclosed by noble mountains, the glen terminates opposite Skye in a lovely bay, along which straggles the picturesque village, embosomed amid scattered timber and overhung by bold metamorphic crags. On the haugh through which the Glenmore River, beloved of salmon fishers, makes its way into the Bay, stand the imposing ruins, well-preserved but totally neglected, of Bernera Barracks, built by the Hanoverian Government in 1722, after the battle of Glenshiel. Here Johnson and Boswell had hoped to stay the night (1st September, 1773) before crossing over to Skye: for, observes Boswell, "soldiers have always everything in the best order." Unfortunately they found only a sergeant and a few men in the place. So they must needs seek quarters in the inn, where "a lass showed us upstairs into a room raw and dirty; bare walls, a variety of bad smells, a coarse black fir greasy table, forms of the same kind, and from a wretched bed started a fellow from his sleep like Edgar in King Lear; 'Poor Tom's a-cold.' " This last unsavoury incident is described by Johnson in his own style: "Out of one of the beds on which we were to repose started up, at our entrance, a man black as a Cyclops from the forge."

About a mile south of Glenelg, but within the parish, opens the parallel smaller valley of Glenbeg. This is a lovely rocky ravine, traversed by a mere farm road, which winds up amid fallen boulders and between rhododendrons, wild roses, wild hyacinths and primroses. It leads us to two of the finest brochs in Scotland, Dun Telve and Dun Troddan, both now carefully preserved by the Ministry of Public Building and Works. Though now in part incomplete, they still stand to a maximum height of some 30 feet. On both sides the hill slopes, rocky above, are finely wooded on the flanks. Altogether, the scenery of Glenbeg must be accounted superb. Still further up is the neolithic chambered cairn of Balvraid, excavated in 1965. But we have now diverged far enough from Skye to give us the requisite glimpse of the ancient gateway of the island.

IV

RAASAY, SCALPAY, AND SOUTH RONA

BETWEEN Skye and the mainland lies the beautiful and interesting island of Raasay, scene of some of the most picturesque passages in Johnson and Boswell's Journals of their famous Tour. From Skye the island is separated by the Sound of Raasay, a little over 5 miles in greatest breadth, and from the Applecross Forest in Ross-shire by the Inner Sound, which at its broadest is about 8 miles in width. The tides in the Sound of Raasay, particularly in the narrows south of Portree, can be very swift. The island is easily accessible from Skye, and Macbrayne's motor vessel calls every weekday except on Thursdays. Raasay measures about 13 miles in length and 3½ miles in greatest breadth. It contains about 27 square miles. To the geologist it offers much varied interest. The northern portion is composed of Lewisian gneiss and Torridonian sandstones; while in the southern part Jurassic sandstones, shales and limestones, in some places richly fossiliferous, predominate, and are overlaid on the higher levels by the great basaltic plateau of Skye. The metamorphic and aqueous sequences are separated by a fault, with a throw of about 1,000 feet, which traverses the island from northeast to south-west—thus following the prevailing trend that marks the geological grain of Scotland. In the Jurassic rocks beds of limestone and ironstone are found, which were intensively mined during the First World War. There are also some oil shales.

Basalt forms the highest summit of the island, Dun Caan (1,456 feet)—otherwise "Raasay's Cap"—upon whose flat top, a miniature version of Macleod's Tables, Boswell, fortified by an *al fresco* breakfast of cold mutton, bread and cheese, brandy and punch, joined with his companions in dancing a Highland reel. From Dun Caan a superb view is obtained over the mainland and Outer Isles. Generally speaking, the island is bare, rocky, grassy

or heath-clad; but there are good cornlands and some thriving,
bird-haunted plantations, particularly around Raasay House, the
former seat of the Macleods of Raasay, where also there is a fine
old walled garden, rich in flowers. Above the house is an artificial
lochan, with several islets clad in rhododendra. Raasay enjoys a
mild climate, and the lushness of its vegetation, whether of forest
trees, shrubs, grasses or flowers, is truly remarkable. The cliff
scenery on the eastern coast is fine, rising sometimes to 1,000
feet; from this side, as in Skye, the surface in general tilts to the
west.

The most interesting antiquity in Raasay is the fantastically
picturesque Castle of Brochel, crowning a small volcanic plug of
Tertiary age—one of three in the northern portion of the island.
All three seem to be the result of single explosions, which blew
out the vents, the orifices being subsequently choked by material
falling from the side walls, so as to form a breccia of Torridonian
sandstones and shales. Brochel Castle was the ancient stronghold
of the Raasay Macleods. It overlooks a beautiful bay on the eastern
side of the island, and consists of what has been aptly described
as "an eyrie-like structure", built on two levels, and to be approached by scrambling rather than climbing. The ruined stronghold fascinated Boswell, who has left a detailed and vivid description of it. He was particularly struck by the fact that it contained
a privy, a convenience lacking in the more modern house where
they were so hospitably entertained. Johnson's comment was:
"you take very good care of one end of a man, but not of the
other!" According to Dean Monro, writing in 1549, Brochel
Castle then possessed "a fair orchard": A wild tradition is told
about the building of the castle, which is ascribed to Ian Mhor
McGillicallum, a cadet of the Dunvegan Macleods. He had become involved in a quarrel with a young chief about the theft of
some dogs, and the dispute ended in the slaughter of the alleged
thief by Ian Mhor's retainer, Gillie-Mhor. In due course the
afflicted father presented himself at Dunvegan, and in the presence
of Ian Mhor and his retainer offered the Chief of the Clan a bag
of silver, to be handed over to anybody who would reveal the
name of his son's slayer. Ian Mhor's henchman at once stepped
forward, boldly avowed the deed, justified the circumstances,
and claimed the reward—which the astonished lord of Dunvegan
duly awarded him. Thereupon the faithful retainer offered the
silver to his master, upon the condition that Ian Mhor would use

the money to build himself a stark strength upon Raasay. Hence in due course the building of Brochel Castle!

Raasay also contains a much dilapidated broch, Dun Borodale, and, near Raasay House, a ruined chapel dedicated to St Moluag of Lismore (see *infra*, pp: 121-2). On the shore beside it is incised a Celtic cross of remarkable design, at which Boswell knelt in prayer. A similar cross, carved on a loose boulder, one of a number formerly on Raasay, is now preserved in the National Museum of Antiquities. Beside Raasay House is one of the few Pictish symbol stones known in the Hebrides (see *supra*, p. 65). It displays the crescent and V-rod and the "tuning fork" symbols below a cross of the peculiar Raasay form. This type of cross, not known elsewhere, is equal armed and of Maltese form, enclosed in a square frame instead of the usual Celtic circle or halo. A vestigial Greek R attached to the cross points to the ultimate derivation of this Raasay group from the famous Chi-Rho monogram, displayed on the sub-Roman early Christian monuments at Whithorn and Kirkmadrine.

The central and oldest portion of Raasay House represents the building where Boswell and Johnson stayed. It was much enlarged in 1773, and since then has been further altered.

Concerning one of the Raasay lochans, Boswell gives us a vivid kelpie legend, related to him, with unquestioning belief, by his informant, Malcolm Macleod, a gentleman of Raasay. The loch contained

a sea-horse which came out and devoured a man's daughter, upon which the man put on a great fire and had a sow roasted at it, the smell of which attracted the monster. The loch was in a hollow between two hills. The fire was placed on the side of the hill to the south-east, a little way down the declivity on that side away from the loch. In the fire was put a spit. The man lay concealed behind a little building of dry stones, and he had an avenue formed for the monster with two rows of large flat stones which reached from the fire over the summit of the hill, till it came on the side next to the loch. The monster came, and the man with the red-hot spit destroyed it. Malcolm showed us the little hiding place and the rows of stones, which seemed to be artificial, though it was not certain.

Prince Charles Edward spent two nights hiding in a shepherd's hut upon Raasay. When a stranger, ostensibly a pedlar of tobacco, approached his lurking place, Raasay and his companion, fearing he might be a spy, proposed to shoot him *instanter.* "God forbid!" said the Prince, "let us not take away a man's life who may be innocent." "Well, well, no matter," rejoined one of the party. "He must be shot. You are the King, but we are the Parliament." Fortunately the stranger passed on without noticing the fugitives. Malcolm Macleod, who had been one of his companions in the hut, told Boswell that the Prince was much broken in his slumber on a couch of heather, crying out in French, Italian and English. On one occasion he exclaimed "O God, poor Scotland!"

As a reward for the devotion of its inhabitants to the Fugitive, the Hanoverian soldiery burned every house upon the island.

Johnson and Boswell were surprised and delighted with their reception in Raasay. Says Johnson: "We found nothing but civility, elegance and plenty . . . More gentleness of manners, or a more pleasing appearance of domestick society, is not found in the most polished countries . . . Such a seat of hospitality, amidst the winds and waters, fills the imagination with a delightful contrariety of images. Without is the rough ocean and the rocky land, the beating billows and the howling storm: within is plenty and elegance, beauty and gaiety, the song and the dance. In Raasay, if I could have found an Ulysses, I had fancied a Phaeacia."

Close south of Raasay, but differing greatly in character from it, is the island of Scalpay. Roughly oval in shape, and some 4¼ miles in greatest diameter, it rises sheer from the sea, tawny and bluff, and consisting simply of a single irregular mass, quite mountainous in aspect though no more than 1,298 feet in height. Mainly it is formed of Torridonian sandstone, but at the south-east corner, round about Scalpay House, is a faulted inlier of fossiliferous Mesozoic rocks, Jurassic and Cretaceous, overlaid by Tertiary basalt. Scalpay is not an island of much scenic prominence, judged by Hebridean standards. Its interest is mainly geological; but it contains, hard by Scalpay House, the ruins of a small Celtic chapel, close to which is a cross-marked slab. The chapel is known as Teampull Fraing. The name *teampull* signifies an early stone church; the second part of the name has been thought to imply a dedication to St Francis.

In the last century the Sound of Scalpay was an assembly point for the herring fleet. It is still noted for its oysters, though this industry is nowadays mainly concentrated at West Loch Tarbert in Argyllshire.

North of Raasay, and virtually a continuation of it—it is separated only by a channel, Kyle Rona, barely half a mile wide—is the small island of South Rona, prolonging the axis of Raasay for a further 4¾ miles, with a maximum breadth of a mile and a quarter. The highest point, Meal Acairseid, is 404 feet. South Rona is composed mainly of Lewisian gneiss (hornblende granulite), much foliated and banded; but in the southern part the Lewisian rocks have been invaded by a remarkable boss of teschenite, so far as exposed at least 1,000 feet in length and over 200 feet in breadth. Teschenite is a basic rock belonging to the dolerite group: the Rona boss is partly columnar, and there can be little doubt that it should be assigned to the Eocene vulcanicity of Skye. A conspicuous feature of the Rona teschenite is the capricious way in which the columnar structure changes direction. Sometimes the columns are vertical, at other times horizontal, while intermediate inclinations are also found. Finely exposed along the eastern coast, the boss is obscured in the interior by peat and heather; but it may be traced in a north-westerly trend as a low ridge between two boggy valleys.

Near the south-eastern corner of the island is *An Teampull*, a small ruined Celtic chapel, well built of rubble and abundant shell-lime. Unfortunately the dedication appears to have been forgotten. In the tiny cemetery no ancient stones are visible.

For the rest, South Rona, though its relief is less bold, differs little in general aspect from the larger island of which it is in effect a prolongation. On the west side is a small harbour, *Acarsaid Thioram*, "Dry Haven", and the northern point of the island carries a lighthouse. As far back as the sixteenth century, South Rona was a notorious haunt of pirates, smugglers, and other such lawless characters: in more recent times it was a favourite lurking place of illicit distillers. There is a wild legend that a Byzantine prince, who had eloped with a daughter of the King of Denmark, was overtaken and slain on South Rona; and that his lover, determined not to survive him, cast herself into his grave, the site of which—*Leac Nighinn Righ Lochlainn*—"the tombstone of the King of Denmark's daughter"—is still pointed out a little to the south of the lighthouse.

At the time of Johnson and Boswell's visit, South Rona was the apanage of the Heir of Raasay, who took his title and derived his income from it. According to Johnson the island then grazed a hundred and sixty head of cattle "under the superintendence of a solitary herdsman", who, it is implied, was then the only human inhabitant.

V

THE SMALL ISLES

Southward from Skye lies the group usually known as the Small Isles, and forming the parish so called. The group numbers four—Canna, Rum, Eigg and Muck. All are in Inverness-shire. The Small Isles are perhaps the most inaccessible and least visited of the Inner Hebrides—though MacBrayne's motor vessel from Kyle and Mallaig to Loch Boisdale calls on Monday, Thursday and Saturday at each of them, Muck excepted. There are no hotels. In the case of Rum, for many years the former owners selfishly discouraged tourists by every means in their power; and now that the island has become a Nature Conservancy, visitors are, for more praiseworthy reasons, not welcomed unless they come on scientific knowledge bent, or in conducted tours organized by the National Trust.

Rum

The largest of the group is the magnificent island of Rum (sometimes spelt Rhum). It forms a roughly circular mass, running out into blunt points on the west and south. Over the two greater diameters, thus formed, the island measures about 8 miles each way. The only significant indent, Loch Scresort, is on the east side. Here is the landing place, overlooked by the pretentious Kinloch Castle, built in 1901 by the former proprietors, and now used by the Nature Conservancy. The red sandstone building stands in well wooded grounds: its material was quarried in Arran. For the most part the coast is rocky, rising in places to sheer precipices, 300 feet in height. The interior of the island forms one superb mountain mass, wild and rugged, culminating in the twin summits of Hallival (2,365 feet) and Askival (2,659 feet). Since the mountains of Rum intercept the rain-laden clouds driving in from the Atlantic, the climate is extremely wet, with the result that there are numerous torrents and waterfalls. On the other hand, there are few lochs, none of any size: the longest, Loch Sgathain, otherwise known as Long Loch, has been harnessed for the needs of Kinloch Castle. The two longest streams are the Kinloch River on the east and the Kilmory River on the north. Their head waters spring quite near each other on comparatively low ground, so that these two river valleys together form a continuous breach in the mountain tangle. There is also an access to the west over Monadh Mhiltich and down Glen Shellesder. Apart from mountain tracks, the only roads connect Kilmory in the north, Kinloch in the east, and Harris in the south-west. At the latter place is the "Grecian" mausoleum of the former proprietors.

The name Rum has been thought pre-Celtic, and to embody the root of the Greek word *rhombos*, in allusion to the island's somewhat lozenge-like shape.

The chief interest in Rum lies in its geology—though, owing to the restrictions above referred to, the island in this respect has so far failed to attract the attention it deserves. The oldest rocks are Torridonian sandstones and shales, which occupy the greater part of the northern sector, prolonged southward along the east coast and lapping round the southern tip. These rocks tilt to the north-west, and in places are ripple-marked. Generally, they tend to form a flattish and somewhat dull landscape. The Torridonians have been much displaced by faulting and overthrusting, so that crush-breccias and mylonites, or crystalline schistose aggregates, are frequent. They have also been further altered by thermal metamorphism due to the Eocene plutonic intrusions. The rest of the island is one huge complex igneous pile; for the mountainous centre of Rum, as stated above (p. 42) is the basal wreck of another of the great chain of Eocene volcanoes that extends up the Atlantic seaboard from Ulster and Arran to Iceland and Greenland. In dealing with Skye I have already set forth in some detail the general sequence of plutonic activity in that island. In Rum it appears to have been broadly the same, except that the oldest or gabbro phase has produced the most ultra-basic suite of rocks in all Britain. As in Skye, the axis of injection and protrusion has shifted; but in Rum not to the east but to the west, where a large mass of granite and granophyre occupies this apex of the island. It rests partly upon the Torridonians and partly upon the basalt poured out in the earlier period of vulcanicity. The granites and granophyres may therefore be regarded as a "laccolite", or bun-shaped intrusion, lifting up the overlying rocks, now almost completely removed by denudation. A feature of the Rum volcano is the series of radiating basic dykes, centred upon the mountain Barkeval (1,924 feet), which itself is a basic mass.

Among the screes at the foot of the truncated crest of the precipitous Sgor Mhor (1,273 feet), otherwise known as Bloodstone Hill, heliotrope, chalcedony and agate may be collected, in the form of amygdaloids fallen out from the vesicles of the basaltic lavas above. Few of the stones, however, owing to impurities, are of any commercial value.

In late Pleistocene times, Rum had its own ice cap, which has left its traces in extensive glaciation of the glens. At the south end of the island, the post-glacial 50 feet raised beach is well displayed, benched into both the Torridonians and the igneous rocks. Generally speaking, the scenery of Rum closely resembles that of the plutonic areas of Skye, and in grandeur is little inferior. As seen from the Point of Sleat or from Strathaird in Skye, from the harbour of Canna, or from Eigg to the south-east, the mass of huge dark, dome-shaped summits, their outlines here and there broken by abrupt escarpments, makes a most striking picture, though nowhere does anything approach the splintered spires of the Cuillins. The hills of Rum, observed Hugh Miller, are "packed closely and squarely together, like rum-bottles in a case-basket."

In the year 1826 the island was occupied by a crofting community of some 400 souls; but in that year all, save one household, were cleared out, lock, stock and barrel, to make way for a single sheep farm. Thus at one fell stroke the population of the island was reduced to a sheep-farmer, a few shepherds, and eight thousand sheep! The resultant desolation is stingingly portrayed by Hugh Miller, who visited Rum in 1845:

The whole of the once peopled interior remains a wilderness, without inhabitant—all the more lonely in its aspect from the circumstance that the solitary valleys, with their plough-furrowed patches, and their ruined heaps of stone, open upon shores every whit as solitary as themselves, and that the wide untrodden sea stretches drearily around. The armies of the insect world were sporting in the light this evening by millions; a brown stream that runs through the valley yielded an incessant poppling sound, from the myriads of fish that were ceaselessly leaping in the pools, beguiled by the quick glancing wings of green and gold that fluttered over them; along a distant hill-side there ran what seemed the ruins of a gray-stone fence, erected, says tradition, in a remote age, to facilitate the hunting of the deer; there were fields upon which the heath and moss of the surrounding moorlands were fast encroaching, that had borne many a successive harvest; and prostrate cottages, that had been the scenes of christenings, and bridals, and blythe new-year's days—all seemed to bespeak the place a fitting habitation for man, in which not only the necessaries but also a few of the luxuries of life, might be procured; but in the entire prospect not a man nor a man's dwelling could the eye command.

A few years after this mass expulsion, some ten or twelve families evicted from Skye were permitted to settle with their cattle beasts on a morass (unsuitable for sheep!) beside Loch Scresort. Today, the island has again a scattered population; but the greater part is now a deer forest. At the Disruption in 1843, three-quarters of the islanders "came out".

The only antiquity in Rum is the ruined church of Kilmory (St Mary's Church) near the mouth of the river named after it, with some ancient stones in its graveyard. Rum was included in the vast territories belonging to the Lady Amy of the Isles, and continued in the grip of her husband, John of Islay, after he divorced her in 1370. In 1373, however, he obtained a Crown charter transferring Rum and Eigg, with North and South Uist, Benbecula and Barra, to his son by Amy, Reginald or Ranald, whose descendants, Clan Ranald, continued to hold Rum until in the eighteenth century it was purchased by MacLean of Coll.

Dr Johnson has preserved to us an amusing story of how the Reformation came to Rum:

> The inhabitants are fifty-eight families, who continued Papists for some time after the Laird became a Protestant. Their adherence to their old religion was strengthened by the countenance of the Laird's sister, a zealous Romanist, till one Sunday, as they were going to mass under the conduct of their patroness, Maclean met them on their way, gave one of them a blow on the head with a "yellow stick", I suppose a cane, for which the Earse had no name, and drove them to the kirk, from which they have never since departed. Since the use of this method of conversion, the inhabitants of Egg and Canna, who continue Papists, call the Protestantism of Rum the religion of the "yellow stick".

As a long-term policy for the island, the Nature Conservancy plan to reintroduce afforestation—between 60 and 70 acres have already been planted—to establish schemes of water conservation, and to stock the island as far as possible with sheep and cattle— while, above all things, preserving its animal and vegetable life in accordance with a balanced pattern. Rum is in fact to become a gigantic outdoor laboratory in order to find out how the Hebrides can best support both wild life and human beings. Particular care is being taken to preserve the island's herd of half-wild ponies.

Canna

Close north-west of Rum, across a bare three miles of turbulent sea, lies the island of Canna, with its eastward tidal appendix, Sanday, connected by a footbridge. In marked contrast to its towering neighbour Rum, Canna consists for the most part of low, green and fertile pasture land: the highest point, Carn a Ghaill, attains an altitude of no more than 690 feet. The total length, including Sanday, may be computed as about five and a half miles; the greatest breadth, somewhat short of three miles. The harbour with its pier is at the eastern end, in the alcove between Canna and Sanday. This is the only pier in the Small Isles alongside which MacBrayne's vessel can berth. As already indicated, Canna is sundered from Sanday at high tide. At no remote period, Canna itself has been two islands; for its central portion consists of a low sandy stretch linking two fine bays, north and south. The southern indent is called Tarbert Bay, and this place name, so frequent in the Highlands and Islands, signifies an isthmus. The slope of the island is from north to south.

Geologically, the island consists of a magnificent suite of terraced basaltic rocks, probably part of the vast outpouring from the Rum volcano. Along the northern coast they build up into mural bastions 600 feet in height. Intercalated with, or traversing the basalts, are thick sheets of columnar dolerite. Whether these are lava flows or intruded sills is a matter of dispute. These igneous rocks overlie conglomerates, amidst which are interstratified patches of ancient soil, containing leaves and stems of fossil plants, including wood charred by the molten lava. The conglomerates include water-worn boulders and pebbles of the older rocks, red Torridonian sandstones and grey foliated gneiss, as well as granite and basalt. These phenomena can only mean that, at the time of the earliest volcanic activity, a river flowed across and eroded the basaltic plateau. Since the conglomerates reach at least 100 feet in thickness, it is clear that this Eocene river must have been both great and powerful. One of the boulders which it transported has been calculated to weigh not less than 12 tons! The presence of gneissose boulders, evidently derived from the Western Highlands, indicates that this long-forgotten river must have flowed from the Inverness-shire mountains across what is now the open sea. In the fantastic stacks along the southern coast of Sanday, no less than four beds of fluviatile sediment are found, separated by lava flows: thus showing, in the clearest fashion, how the course of the river was repeatedly interrupted by fresh volcanic outbursts.

On Compass Hill, at the eastern end of Canna, the basalt is highly magnetic, so as greatly to disturb the compasses (at least it is averred) of vessels plying offshore. At the east end of Compass Hill, low down above the foreshore, and extending southward into the lofty stack of Coroghon Mor, a mass of volcanic agglomerate evidently fills up a major eruptive vent.

Archaeologically, as befits a far more fertile island, Canna is much richer ground than its big neighbour Rum. Burial cairns, standing stones, *duns* and earthhouses take us back to prehistoric times. At least four Viking graves have been identified. On the site of St Columba's Chapel at A'Chill, north of the post office, stands a much mutilated high cross of early type, with human and animal figures, including a horse and its rider of Pictish rather than Hebridean character. A grave slab in the same cemetery is of the more usual West Highland type, but marked by a bizarre collection of portrayals. In the Memorial Church—a conspicuous structure with its round tower, built in 1914—is preserved another enriched cross-shaft. The well-preserved ruins of a monastic cashel, with its interior buildings, invite excavation upon the foreshore below Am Beannan, on the southern coast of the island. Its Gaelic name, Sgor nam Ban-naomha, signifies "the Skerry of the Holy Women", whence it may be inferred that the establishment had been a nunnery. Sundered from the land by basalt escarpments, and approachable from the sea only in calm weather, it seems an ideal spot for holy recluses. Lastly, there is the fragmentary castle ruin on Coroghon Mor. This is

> Canna's tower, that, steep and gray,
> Like falcon-nest o'erhangs the bay

concerning which Scott, in *The Lord of the Isles*, relates a pathetic story of how a jealous Lord confined for life in this lonely eyrie

Isle of Rum from Glendale, Eigg

a young and lovely bride from foreign parts. Her restless spirit
still haunts the lonely stack:

> And still, when on the cliff and bay
> Placid and pale the moonbeams play,
>   And every breeze is mute,
> Upon the lone Hebridean's ear,
> Steals a strange pleasure mix'd with fear,
> While from that cliff he seems to hear
>   The murmur of a lute,
> And sounds, as of a captive lone,
> That mourns her woe in tongue unknown.

Many of the inhabitants are Catholic, and worship in their own
chapel on Sanday.

Eigg

In some ways the most interesting of the Small Isles is Eigg.
To begin with, this island enjoys a literary glamour all its own
among the group, owing to the visit in 1845 of Hugh Miller,
who in that grand book *The Cruise of the Betsey*, has consecrated
some of his most brilliant descriptive eloquence to the scenic
glories and unique geological interest of Eigg. The circumstances
of Hugh Miller's visit are themselves romantic enough. His life-
long friend, the Rev. John Swanson, Minister of the Small Isles,
with the majority of his congregation "came out" in the Disruption. Inevitably he lost his church and manse. Most of the insular
lairds of his parish adhered to the Established Church; and so
bitter had been the feelings aroused in the prolonged dispute
which ended by splitting the Church of Scotland, that none of
these proprietors would give the dispossessed minister a house
to live in, nor his scattered congregation a site to build themselves a church and manse. Reduced thus to heroic poverty, the
indomitable minister obtained a small yacht, which during the
summer season he made his home, and amid all the perils of the
western seas, ministered to his island flock, preaching where he
could, in "black houses" or in the open air. Himself an expert
seaman, the minister had a crew of only one in all his dangerous
voyaging. Whatever opinion may be held about the rights and
wrongs of the Disruption, nothing but admiration can be felt
for such self-sacrificing devotion, and for the staunch loyalty of
the faithful who clung to their dispossessed pastor. As Editor of

7

The Sgurr of Eigg

The Witness, Hugh Miller was one of the leading lay champions in Scotland of the struggling Free Kirk. Moreover, he was an old friend of Mr Swanson's. In both these capacities, and not least as an ardent geologist, he welcomed the minister's invitation to join him in his summer cruise among the Small Isles. It resulted in one of the most brilliant books in early geological literature— marked on every page by Christian piety, scientific enthusiasm, deep philosophical reflection, and above all, mastery of the English tongue.

Miller has set down his first impression of Eigg, as the *Betsey* approached the island, in the following terms. The island struck him as

resembling in outline two wedges placed point to point on a board. The centre is occupied by a deep angular gap, from which the ground slopes upward on both sides, till, attaining its extreme height at the opposite ends of the island, it drops suddenly on the sea. In the northern rising ground the wedge-like outline is complete; in the southern one it is somewhat modified by the gigantic Scuir, which rises direct on the apex of the height, *i.e.* the thick part of the wedge; and which, seen bows-on from this point of view, resembles some vast donjon-keep, taller from base to summit, by about a hundred feet, than the dome of St. Paul's. The upper slopes of the island are brown and moory, and present little on which the eye may rest, save a few trap terraces with rudely columnar fronts; its middle space is mottled with patches of green, and studded with dingy cottages, each of which this morning, just a little before the breakfast hour, had its own blue cloudlet of smoke diffused around it; while along the beach, patches of level sand, alternated with tracts of green bank, or both, give place to stately ranges of basaltic columns, or dingy groups of detached rocks. Immediately in front of the central hollow, as if skilfully introduced to relieve the tamest part of the prospect, a noble wall of semicircular columns rises some eighty or a hundred feet over the shore; and on a green slope, directly above, we see the picturesque ruins of the Chapel of St. Donan, one of the disciples of Columba, and the Culdee saint and apostle of the island.

Like every visitor to Eigg, Miller was struck by the extreme whiteness of its shelly sands. He also gives us the first account of its famous "musical sands", at Camas Sgiotaig, towards the north-west end of the island. These, formed almost entirely of quartzose grains, when trodden upon yield "a shrill sonorous note, somewhat resembling that produced by a waxed thread, when tightened between the teeth and the hand, and tipped by the nail of the fore-finger." For the rest, apart from his brilliant description of the scenic and geological character of the island, the chief interest in Hugh Miller's chapters upon Eigg consists in his account of the touching devotion of the dispossessed pastor and his congregation to each other. Before the Disruption Mr Swanson had built, out of his own pocket, "a low dingy cottage of turf and stone, situated nearly opposite to the manse windows". This had been intended for a Gaelic school. Though he had forfeited the manse, the minister of course retained possession of his cottage; and in this humble building the Sunday service was held. Though the rain was pouring, the little hut was packed out. Of course the sermon was in Gaelic, but "my friend, at the conclusion of his discourse, gave a brief digest of its contents in English, for the benefit of his one Saxon auditor". The whole occasion made a powerful impression upon Miller's pious and ardent mind:

There was as little of the reverence of externals in the place as can well be imagined: an uneven earthen floor—turf walls on every side, and a turf roof above—two little windows of four panes apiece, adown which the rain-drops were coursing thick and fast—a pulpit grotesquely rude, that had never employed the bred carpenter—and a few ranges of seats of undressed deal—such were the mere materialisms of this lowly church of the people; and yet here, notwithstanding, was the living soul of a Christian community—understandings convinced of the truth of the Gospel, and hearts softened and impressed by its power.

The island of Eigg lies some 4 miles south-east of Rum. It measures 6½ miles in length, from north to south, by 4 miles greatest breadth. On the west side its rocky coast, pierced by many a chasm and cave, is indented by the broad bay of Laig. The highest point (1,289 feet) is the famous Sgurr, one of the most remarkable geological features and most striking pieces of inland cliff scenery in Britain. The harbour of Eigg is at Galmisdale, on the south-east side—a mere embayment in an open tideway, but sheltered by Eilean Chathastail, on which are the remains of a *dun*.

Despite its lack of size and fertility, Eigg is an island of consider-able historical and antiquarian interest. It is mentioned, under its existing name—*Egea insula*—in Adamnan's *Life of St Columba*. The name is said to signify the "island of the notch", in allusion doubtless to the "deep angular gap", as Hugh Miller calls it, that traverses the island from Laig to Kildonan. In the annals of the Celtic Church, the name of Eigg is forever associated with the martyrdom of St Donnan, who founded a monastery on the island, and with fifty-two of his brethren, met his death at the hands of pirates on Easter Sunday, 16th April, 618. In the old Irish annals conflicting accounts have been preserved about the tragedy. According to the *Martyrology of Donegal*:

> There came robbers of the sea on a certain time to the island, when he was celebrating mass. He requested of them not to kill him until he should have the mass said, and they gave them this respite; and he was afterwards beheaded, and fifty-two of his monks along with him.

Other accounts aver that the number martyred was a hundred and fifty, and that they were burned—doubtless by setting the church on fire over their heads. But a gloss in the *Martyrology of Oengus* ascribes the catastrophe to the offended proprietorial instincts of a local chieftainess:

> Donnan then went with his people to the Hebrides; and they took up their abode there, in a place where the sheep of the queen of the country were kept. This was told to the queen. "Let them all be killed!" said she. "That would not be a religious act," said her people. But they were murderously assailed. At this time the cleric was at mass. "Let us have respite till mass is ended," said Donnan. "Thou shalt have it," said they. And when it was over, they were slain, every one of them.

> With the festival of Peter the Deacon
> To glorious martyrdom ascended
> With his clerics of pure lives
> Donnan of cold Eigg.

One old Irish account has preserved a list of the fifty-two monks who thus perished with their abbot, St Donnan. Their names should be inscribed upon a tablet somewhere on the island.

Nine centuries or thereby after the tragedy of St Donnan, another ghastly massacre took place on Eigg. It has left an indelible impression on the memories of the Western Islanders. The Macdonalds of Eigg, like the rest of their clan, were in bitter feud with the Macleods. On one occasion, so the story goes, the inhabitants of Eigg had, with true Celtic hospitality in spite of their clan enmity, afforded shelter and entertainment to a party of Macleods stranded upon the island. Unfortunately one of these involuntary visitors offered an incivility to a girl of the island; whereupon the Macdonalds seized their guests, bound them, and set them adrift in an open boat. When the news was brought to Macleod of Macleod, he manned his galleys and set forth from Loch Follart to wreak his vengeance upon the inhabitants of Eigg. Warned of his arrival, the entire population sought refuge in a cave by the shore. The Macleods on landing found the island apparently deserted, and were preparing to depart, when one of them caught sight of a Macdonald who incautiously had left his refuge to reconnoitre. As a light snow had fallen, his footsteps were traced back to the cave. Since the wind was blowing in from the sea, the ruthless Macleod kindled a huge bonfire at its mouth, and the entire population of the island, men, women and bairns, said to number a couple of hundred, were smoked to death.

Whatever may be the truth about the details of this horrific story, there seems to be no doubt concerning the essential fact of the massacre. It is confirmed by the evidence of the cave, which has yielded many miserable relics of the victims. The cave, Uamh Fhraing, is at the southern extremity of the island. Hugh Miller has given us a vivid and poignant description of what he found there. It deserves to be quoted *in extenso*:

The floor, for about a hundred feet inwards from the narrow vestibule, resembles that of a charnel house. At almost every step we come upon heaps of human bones grouped together, as the Psalmist so graphically described, "as when one cutteth and cleaveth wood upon the earth." They are of a brownish, earthy hue, here and there tinged with green; the skulls, with the exception of a few broken fragments, have disappeared; for travellers in the Hebrides have of late years been numerous and curious; and many a museum—that at Abbotsford among the rest—exhibits, in a grinning skull, its memorial of the Massacre at Eigg. We find, too, further marks of visitors in the single bones separated from the heaps and scattered over the area; but still enough remains to show, in the general disposition of the remains, that the hapless islanders died under the walls in families, each little group separated by a few feet from the others.[1] Here and there the remains of a detached skeleton may be seen, as if some robust islander, restless in his agony, had stalked out into the middle space ere he fell; but the social arrangement is the

[1] It is interesting to note that in 1773 Dr. Johnson was told how the people smothered in the cave were left "lying dead by families as they stood".

general one. And beneath every heap we find . . . the remains of
the straw-bed upon which the family had lain, largely mixed with
the smaller bones of the human frame, ribs and vertebrae, and hand
and feet bones; occasionally, too, with fragments of unglazed
pottery, and various other implements of a rude housewifery.

In an adjoining cave, after the Rising of 1745, when the
ancient faith, to which most of the islanders adhered, was
persecuted, the priest of Eigg ministered to his flock—thus antici-
pating, at the opposite pole of Christian witness, the equal con-
stancy of the Free Kirk minister of a hundred years later. Sir
Walter Scott, who visited Uamh Fhraing in 1814, and (as Hugh
Miller relates) carried off with him a skull, tells us about this other
cave that "a huge ledge of rocks, rising about halfway up one
side of the vault, served for altar and pulpit; and the appearance
of a priest and Highland congregation in such an extraordinary
place of worship, might have engaged the pencil of Salvator."
Scott gives the dimensions of Uamh Fhraing as 255 feet in length,
and 18 or 20 feet in greatest breadth and height.

The antiquities of Eigg include a *dun* on top of the Sgurr—
possibly the "most impressive fort site in Scotland"; three Viking
graves, containing the usual swords, buckles, belt-mountings,
brooches and so forth, and in one case a necklace of amber and
jet; and the ruined church of St Donnan, with four cross-shafts
or grave slabs of the customary Hebridean type.

But the prime interest of Eigg, beyond doubt, resides in its
geology. For its size, the island has perhaps as large a literature in
this subject as any locality in Scotland. The oldest rocks are
Jurassic. These back upon the Bay of Laig, and lap round the
northern and eastern coastlines of the island. They have yielded
a rich assemblage of fossils, including remains of the fantastic
reptiles of that ancient time, among them the airborne Pterodactyl.
Hugh Miller, who discovered these beds, has given us a thrilling
account of his explorations. How strange it is to conceive the
picture, yielded by these fossils, of conditions in the area now
occupied by the Small Isles, some hundred and fifty millions of
years ago, when uncouth reptiles were the lord of creation, and
the first mammals, heirs of the future, were mere rat-like creatures, feeding on small fruits and insects!

Among the Jurassic rocks of Eigg perhaps the most singular
feature is the bands of hard concretionary masses that occur at

two levels in the softish sandstones. When weathered out, particularly on the underside of an overhanging shelf of rock, they have been likened to a series of huge wasps' nests. When upright on a rock ledge, they are compared by Hugh Miller to a field of petrified gigantic mushrooms.

At Clach Alasdair, near the west end of Laig Bay, a patch of Upper Cretaceous rocks has been identified. For the rest, the rocks of Eigg belong to the grand period of Tertiary plutonic activity. In general sequence and character they correspond with the terraced basaltic plateau areas of Skye, and therefore need not be here discussed in detail. Something, however, must be said about the famous Sgurr of Eigg. This astonishing feature—alike from near and far the landmark of the island—may be described as a vast prow of black glassy columnar pitchstone, 500 yards in breadth, 400 feet or thereby in height, and in its sinuous length measuring a couple of miles, or maybe a little more. It has been fully investigated by Sir Archibald Geikie, who described it as "one of the most impressive monuments of denudation to be found within the British Islands." Sometimes the pitchstone columns are horizontal; elsewhere they are slantwise; in some cases they appear, as Geikie remarks, to be piled together like a peat-stack. This pitchstone ridge is set in a deep V-shaped hollow of the underlying terraced basalt: but between the two igneous rocks, at the base of this sealed up valley, is a band of shingle, containing many fragments of wood. Sir Archibald accordingly inferred that the pitchstone, which varies in composition, represented a series of lava-flows pouring down an ancient river valley and sealing up its pebble beds together with the fragments of trees brought down by the current. The stream might perhaps be regarded as a tributary of the great Eocene river whose traces we noticed in Canna—if indeed it was not a separate channel of that river. Other geologists have interpreted the Sgurr as an intrusive mass; but Sir Archibald's classic and imaginative explanation still finds its authoritative champions.

From the north-west side the Sgurr can be fairly easily climbed; and the visitor who makes the effort will be rewarded, if the day be clear, by a superb prospect of the Small Isles, Skye, and the embattled crests of Ardnamurchan and Kintail.

The island has been heavily glaciated, the striations and travelled boulders indicating a general movement from west to east. Many of the boulders are derived from the mainland. As is often the case in areas which have been subjected to a general ice-sheet rather than to local glaciation, the island boasts few lakes, though a fair number of tarns.

Eigg is still the seat of the parish church and manse of the Small Isles, though its crofting population has much diminished since the beginning of the present century. I believe it now numbers about 80. The best land is found on the Jurassic rocks. Many of the people retain their allegiance to the ancient faith, and are served by a chapel.

Muck

Little need here be said about the small island of Muck, which is not a calling point for MacBrayne's motor vessels. Lying within three miles south of Eigg, the islet measures not much more than two miles either way. Low, green and fertile, it supports a small crofting community, whose wealth consists in sheep and potatoes. Its ancient name was Eilean nam Muc, Swine Island, which seems to indicate its long established agricultural importance. In the sixteenth century it is described as "very fertill and fruitful of cornes and grassing for all store, and very guid for fishing, inhabit and manurit, a good falcon nest in it." The rocks belong in the main to the Tertiary igneous suite, but Jurassic beds, of considerable thickness and containing oysters and other fossil shells, as well as fish scales, are exposed on the shore of Camas Mor, the chief bay on the southern coast. The island presents a fine field for the study of intrusive basic dykes, which on the fore-shore sometimes stand out like a series of parallel ruinous sea-walls. These dykes traverse the island from north-west to south-east, as if heading out from the Rum volcano. On this low island, in marked contrast to Canna and Eigg, glacial drift has accumulated, a fact to which its fertility is doubtless partly due. As we shall find in the Outer Isles, the soil is also enriched by wind-blown shell-sand, which acts the part of a natural marl manure.

The Small Isles belonged to Clanranald, and as such were pitilessly ravaged by Sir Lachlan Mor Maclean of Duart in 1588—with the aid, it is told, of Spanish soldiers rescued from the galleon *Florida*, which sank in Tobermory Bay. The whole population of the islands is said to have been exterminated.

VI

LEWIS AND HARRIS

Although they differ widely in scenery, and administratively belong to two different counties, Lewis and Harris geographically form a unit—the largest in the Long Island, and indeed the largest and most populous of the Hebrides—in fact, next to the British mainland and Ireland, the largest of the Britannic Isles. Moreover, Lewis is the only one among the Hebrides that in Stornoway boasts a town. Together Lewis and Harris measure 59 miles in length, and about 20 miles in greatest breadth. The population, which for the time being appears to be static, may be computed as about 23,000: in 1901, it was nearly 34,300. What may be regarded as the geographical division between the two portions of "the Lews", as the island is collectively and colloquially styled, is the narrow isthmus between East and West Lochs Tarbert, two fiords which betwixt them reduce the island to a span of under a mile. Administratively, the boundary lies further north, from Loch Seaforth in the east to Loch Resort in the west. North of this is Lewis proper, belonging to Ross-shire, whilst all to the south, as far as the Sound of Harris, is part of Inverness-shire.

Topographically, the division is as sharp as could be. Both portions of the island are composed, almost entirely, of Lewisian gneiss, a formation more than once already alluded to in these pages. Here we find its greatest and classic development in the island which has given this famous formation its name. These profoundly altered rocks, orthogneisses and paragneisses, are, it may well be, the oldest and toughest of all the many layers in the gnarled complex hide of our venerable Mother Earth. But whereas in Lewis the surface is in general low, flat and moorish, Harris rises into high rocky mountains, culminating in North Harris—the portion above Tarbert—in the grand peak of The Clisham (2,622 feet).

I doubt very much if, for its size, there is any town in Britain that quite resembles Stornoway. Though it boasts just over 5,000 inhabitants, it has about it a metropolitan, one might even say a cosmopolitan air, and is pervaded by a sense of bustle, energy, self-confidence and *élan*, which you will seek in vain elsewhere in the easy-going Hebrides. Though the herring industry is no longer what it once was, the town is still a considerable fishing port; and during the season its capacious and well-equipped harbour is thronged with the vessels of many nations, while, in the crowded streets of the little town divers tongues assail your ear in addition to the euphonious Gaelic of the indwellers. Great efforts are being made to foster the fishing industry; the chief obstacle is the lack of facilities for processing the fish. Stornoway is also famed, all the world over, as a centre of the Harris tweed industry. It is the principal shopping market in the Outer Isles, and has laid itself out, with no small success, as a tourist centre— for both the town and the island of which it is the capital have much to offer the visitor, be he geologist, naturalist, antiquary, mountaineer, sportsman, golfer, or merely a sightseer. There is a most enthusiastic Sea Angling Club, and a Pipe Band with a wizard record of fund-raising. In Lews Castle, Stornoway possesses a first-class technical college, and in the Nicolson Institute a secondary school of whose roll of honour Lewis, indeed all Scotland, has reason to be proud. The material comforts of visitors are looked after by six hotels and numerous boarding houses. In the Eye peninsula, east of the town, is the island's first-class airport, a legacy of the last war, connecting with Renfrew (for Glasgow) and Inverness, while MacBrayne's motor vessel, equipped for transporting cars, calls twice daily (except on Sundays) from Mallaig.

A remarkable feature about Stornoway is its Pakistani community. These immigrants came to the island after the Second World War. They have prospered modestly in trade, and have become thoroughly integrated with the Celtic community. Some have even mastered Gaelic, and in the peat mosses outside the town you may see a Pakistani and a Hebridean working side by side, each on his "lair", and conversing in the ancient tongue of the Gael. Another noteworthy feature about this fascinating town is the firm of James Mackenzie and Sons Ltd., which deals in furniture, kitchen utensils and china. This business is managed as a benevolent trust, its profits having been assigned for behoof of aged and infirm persons within the burgh.

Situated at the head of a capacious land-locked basin, sheltered on either side by Holm Point and Arnish Point, Stornoway must surely have been the site of a fishing community long before it became a staging point for the Norse galleys on their way to the Inner Isles, Man and Ireland. The name of the town is Norse, and is said to mean "Anchor Bay". Its castle appears first on record in the sixteenth century, during which it had a stormy history. Finally it was destroyed by Cromwell's troops, but some fragments survived until 1882. The site, on a rock overlooking the foreshore, is now marked by a flagstaff and a plaque upon an adjoining wall, commemorating the *quondam* castle in Gaelic and English. To replace it, but on a different stance, the Protectorate government built a fort, to guard the harbour from the hostile attentions of Dutch privateers during Cromwell's war with the Netherlands. Like the castle, the Cromwellian fort is now a thing of the past. In 1637 Stornoway was erected into a royal burgh: but it remained a struggling fisherman's village until the material requisites for its development as a natural fishing centre were provided by Sir James Matheson, of whom more hereafter.

The older part of the burgh is picturesquely grouped upon "the Point" and along the east side of the inner basin of the harbour, which, with its constant bustle afloat and ashore, and the ceaseless clangour of the seafowl, is as fascinating a place as harbours always are. Across the narrow water is the imposing pile of Lews Castle, standing amid spacious grounds whose fine sycamore woodlands come as a surprise to the visitor who expects to land upon a treeless island. In spring, the display of rhododendrons has few equals in Scotland. In the dells and crannies grow hazel, creeping willow and honeysuckle, and in spring and summer the green grass is spangled with woodland flowers. Behind the older quarter of the town its modern extension, spaciously planned as a gridiron of streets, climbs the slopes to the east. Every newcomer to Stornoway must be struck with the number of large, solidly constructed houses, each in its well-tended garden. Clearly this is a town where prosperity is not unknown. It need hardly be added that the burgh possesses the usual plethora of churches, inseparable from the Scottish scene.

Lews castle was completed in 1870, at the huge cost, for that period, of £70,000. Built of local stone, with imported white freestone dressings, it is in the heavy castellated Tudor Gothic

style, fashionable in mid-Victorian times; and, as originally designed, contained no less than 76 rooms. The policies, upon which
a further £50,000 was expended, included 10 miles of drives
and 5 miles of footpaths. Even today, reduced and simplified as
are the grounds, the *ensemble*, castle and policies, strikes the be-
holder with astonishment in this remote and desolate island.
Lews Castle—or Stornoway Castle as for a time it used to be
called—was built, and the grounds laid out, by a distinguished
Highlander, a native of Sutherland, Sir James Matheson, Bt., who
had made a fortune as a tea merchant in the Far East. He purchased Lewis in 1844, for the sum of £190,000 and from first to
last is said to have laid out £574,000 on the improvement of his
property. In particular, he modernized the port and town of
Stornoway; but his benevolent enterprises extended into every
corner of the island. Schools were built, old roads repaired and
new roads laid out, thousands of acres of land reclaimed, and
stock and seed improved. On the reverse side of the medal,
crofters were evicted to make way for sheep and deer; and so the
inhabitants of Lewis played their part in the unrest that led to
the appointment of the Crofters Commission in 1884.

In 1918 Lewis was bought from Colonel Duncan Matheson
by Lord Leverhulme. Once again the island was in the hands of
a "rich man furnished with ability". Next year, in two gulps, he
purchased Harris, so that now, as the sole proprietor of the whole
island, with its 570,000 acres, he became the largest landowner in
Britain. The record of Viscount Leverhulme's colossal effort to
modernize Lewis and Harris, and to turn their inhabitants into
a viable community, as he understood it; his vast expenditure on
all his many projects—estimated to have reached a total of
£1,400,000; and his final disillusionment and failure, make up a
story at once heroic and tragic, and one which casts a searchlight
beam on the psychological problem that lies at the very root of
the economic *malaise* of the Hebrides. The tale has been brilliantly
told in a recent study,[1] and concerns us here no more than for
the insight which it gives us into the character and outlook of
the island populace.

Sir James Matheson's efforts had been mainly directed to the
improvement of his broad acres. By contrast, Lord Leverhulme's
eyes were firmly fixed upon the sea. He could envisage no future
in crofting:

[1] Nigel Nicolson, *Lord of the Isles*, 1960.

At the present time you see young men leaving the island to es-
cape poverty; you see children watching cattle all the live-long day
on the wind-swept grazings; you see women carrying creels of peat
on their backs, a weight of 80 lbs, while in the Congo no negro
woman is allowed by law to carry more than 44 lbs; and you see
the men coming back from the sea with fish that must either be
consumed in the village or salted and packed in barrels—the least
remunerative way of selling that hard-won harvest. These people
are not adding to their happiness. They are merely existing.

The great wealth of Lewis is in the surrounding sea, and not in
the land. The only recovery, it seems to me, can be reaping the
harvest of the sea and establishing industries in the island; and so
gradually find employment for the people, apart altogether from
their small crofts, out of which it would be impossible under any
circumstances whatever, even freed of all payments of rents or rates,
for the people to make a living. On the other hand, out of the
harvest of the sea there ought to be a basis for solid prosperity in
the island.

Upon these principles, clearly thought out in advance, and
soundly based upon a close study of his predecessor's achievements and failures, Lord Leverhulme addressed himself, with
idealism, imagination and indomitable persistence, to his self-
imposed gigantic task. In background, ingrained habit of mind,
and experience, he was poles apart from the Gaelic peasantry
whose lot he sought with passionate earnestness to improve. But
if he knew little or nothing of the Hebrides, he could buy expert
advice. Above all, he possessed a high intelligence, complete
integrity and a stalwart will. At the very outset of his dramatic
intervention in "the Lews", he testified, in the warmest terms,
to his appreciation of "the charm and attraction of its people."
He was forcibly struck by the fact that the Lewismen, who on
their own island seemed condemned, by slavish adherence to
what he regarded as an obsolete, penurious way of life, to protract
their existence from generation unto generation "under conditions of squalor and misery"—these same Lewismen, when they
emigrated into wider spheres of action, had won for themselves
competence, affluence, and even renown throughout the English-
speaking world. Moreover, these same backward Lewismen had
furnished one-sixth of their entire population for service in the
war; and in the course of it had lost upwards of 1,100 dead—
a tragic total that has been claimed as "perhaps the heaviest
proportionate loss in the Empire". In Leverhulme's view, the

solution to this dichotomy was basically simple: to divert the
energies of the islanders from crofting to fishing, and the introduction, or development, of industry—in particular, the modern-
ization and expansion of the traditional industry of weaving. No
reasonable student of this extraordinary episode in Hebridean
history can doubt that essentially Lord Leverhulme was right.
Unfortunately he failed to appreciate the age-long hunger of the
islander for land—for a holding of his own, be it ever so small,
and although the living to be scraped from such poor and narrow
acres must be modest in the extreme. Nor could he foresee the
impact upon the island of the returning ex-service men—no
longer now backward peasants of the "Celtic fringe", but steel-
hardened men whose impressions of other lands had been tem-
pered in the fires of a world-wide war. Coming back to Lewis,
these men demanded crofts. Leverhulme had pinned his faith
upon farms, fishing and industry. The misfortune is that there
was ample room on the island for both. The ex-service men
could have had all the crofts they wanted, without prejudice to
Leverhulme's desire to encourage farming and fishing.

Two circumstances combined to make the resultant controversy
all the more pitiful. In the first place, here was a landlord, with
vast wealth at his command, whose sole and declared purpose
was the economic betterment of his tenantry:

> Of course it would be impossible to develop Lewis commercially,
> put railways through the island, construct docks and harbours,
> place herring canneries, and at the same time maintain the sporting
> attractions of the island, but my instincts lean towards men and
> women and not to salmon and grouse and deer, and if the interests
> of the two clash, the salmon and deer must go.

In the second place, it cannot be too strongly emphasized that
so far as the evidence goes, the overwhelming majority of Lewismen supported their new laird's grandiose plans for the island.
The opposition came, overtly at all events, from a comparatively
small number of ex-service men, returning, as most of them did
in 1919, with scant respect for authority, habituated to strong
action, and determined, by violence if need be, to secure for themselves small-holdings in their native island. No one need with-
hold acknowledgment of the deep well-springs of emotion,
drawing their sources from a remote past, upon which this
passionate land-hunger was based. The "green land of their fore-

fathers" was something in which these men felt that their service and their sacrifice had earned them a stake. Moreover, the Government had promised it them. So far back as 1917 the Lord Advocate had pledged that, after the war, "the land question in the Highlands should be settled once and for all", and that "the people of the Highlands must be placed in possession of the soil". Nevertheless, the ex-servicemen who in 1919 seized land in the Lews, driving off the farmers' cattle and sheep and pulling down dykes and fences, did not enjoy the approbation of the vast majority of Lewismen—at least so far as we can judge from their public condemnation of such violence. After all, Lord Lever-hulme's enterprises were bringing undreamt prosperity to the island. The wages bill on his public works alone was running at about £2,500 a week. Yet the Highland character is a subtle one, and evidence is not lacking that in their secret hearts not a few among the islanders sympathized with the land-grabbers.

In 1919 Lord Leverhulme was a man of eight and sixty years. His mind was deeply scored with the impressions of an unparal-leled business career; his instincts of paternal despotism strength-ened by his achievements at Port Sunlight and in the Congo. Violence and lawlessness he could not away with; and his resent-ment at the raiders was blown to white heat by the overt support lent to their law-breaking by the Secretary for Scotland, who allowed Lord Leverhulme to understand that if the raiders were jailed by the courts, he would forthwith order their release. Further head-on conflict arose from the Scottish Secretary's determination to acquire, by compulsory purchase and for turn-ing into crofts, farms in the environs of Stornoway, which in Lever-hulme's judgment were essential to his plans for supplying the town with milk produced in Lewis, instead of importing it expensively from Easter Ross and Aberdeenshire.

Hard upon these accumulated tensions came the great post-war slump, and the collapse of the continental herring market upon which Leverhulme had so largely built his hopes. To add to his difficulties, now for the first time in his life he found himself con-fronted with financial stringency, both in the vast Lever Brothers consortium and in his private commitments. So in 1921, under conditions of extreme mental stress, he abandoned all his immense undertakings in Lewis. Those in Harris he continued, including the establishment of a fishing port at Obbe, rechristened Lever-burgh. But when on 10th May, 1925, death terminated Viscount

Leverhulme's astonishing career, these enterprises were speedily wound up. Today in Lewis and Harris little remains of all this vast and manifold development save uncompleted housing schemes at Stornoway and Leverburgh; bridges and roads, some of the latter unfinished; and the furtive regrets of an island populace who have not bothered to erect a monument to their greatest benefactor. "The ruling passion of his life," wrote a member of his staff, "was not money or even power, but the desire to increase human wellbeing by substituting the profitable for the valueless." How true is this verdict will be understood from the fact that when Leverhulme abandoned Lewis he created the Stornoway Trust, handing over to this body—in which the Town Council are *ex officio* members and are accompanied by elected representatives from the landward area—not only Stornoway Castle and grounds, but much other property in and around the burgh. Since it was established, the Stornoway Trust has done much to further the interests of the town and its environs.

To some small degree, one aspect of Leverhulme's work was carried on by the Macaulay Institute for Soil Research, founded in 1928 by a distinguished Canadian of Lewis stock, Dr T. B. Macaulay. At Arnish, three miles south of Stornoway, the Institute, whose headquarters are now in Aberdeen, for long maintained a demonstration farm, chiefly devoted to the reclamation of peat.

The Lewis peat mosses are of vast extent, and in places reach a depth of 20 feet. Most of the peat is highly acid, and poor in plant food substances. Peat cutting regulations, such as are enforced in the Baltic countries, are unknown in the Hebrides. Thus over much of the surface in Lewis, notably around the crofting townships, the peat has been "skinned", exposing the native rock or sterile boulder clay. Such land is of course useless alike for grazing or cultivation. The experiments conducted at Arnish foundered upon the problem of drainage. After some seventy acres had been reclaimed for cultivation or grazing, the area with its buildings had to be let to a tenant; the farm passed out of cultivation, and the remainder is now used for grazing dairy cows.

As an instance of the special difficulties that beset the cultivator in Lewis, owing to the softness of the ground at Arnish a special form of tractor with very broad wheels, or rather drum-like attachments, was brought in from Sweden.[1] Nevertheless, some

[1] This machine may be described as a fast-revolving horizontal shaft furnished with bent steel knives, which shred the surface of the peat.

Part of Stornoway, Lewis

useful results were obtained from the experiments at Arnish: notably that the peat soils benefit far more from organic manures —seaweed or farmyard dung—than from chemicals. Turnips, carrots and kail did moderately well, though the shallow tillage was a handicap. Yet the scientists hopefully concluded that "with better tilth and suitable manuring many crops could be grown successfully on Lewis peat." Of dairy pasturage, grass and clover did much better than rye. Experiments in the reclamation of "skinned" land failed to yield promising results. Altogether, the problem of peat reclamation in Lewis is thus seen to be an intractable one. Nevertheless, under the direction of the North of Scotland College of Agriculture, some 11,000 acres of heath-land have been converted into pasture; so that whereas in 1956 no fat sheep or cattle were graded at Stornoway, in 1964 15,000 fat sheep and 1,100 fat cattle were graded there.

Thomas Basset Macaulay, the founder of the Institute that bears his name, was President of the Sun Life Assurance Company of Canada. Descended from the Macaulays of Uig, he was a notable benefactor to the islands of his ancestors. He endowed the Stornoway Public Library, contributed largely to the building of the new Town Hall, and founded the Macaulay Education Trust.

The Macaulays are a clan settled in Lewis at least since the early years of the seventeenth century. One of them, the Rev. John Macaulay, Minister at South Uist, has the unsavoury distinction of having betrayed the secret that Prince Charles Edward was lurking in the Long Island. He told his father, the Rev. Aulay Macaulay, Minister at Harris, who passed the information on to a Presbyterian lay preacher. The Rev. John Macaulay, it is interesting to note, was the grandfather of Lord Macaulay, who doubtless owed his Whig bias to his ancestry. In this of course there was nothing discreditable; but it is less easy to understand how, with his Celtic ancestry, the great historian should have presented his readers, in his famous thirteenth chapter, with so gross a caricature of the Scottish Highlanders.

Since the herring industry has entered upon a long, though let us hope not a lasting decline, the chief occupation of Lewis, encouraged in every way by the Government, continues to be the crofting in which Leverhulme could see no future. Farms have been broken up into crofts, and the process of re-housing the crofters in the neat white up-to-date cottages, which we have noticed elsewhere, is in active progress both in Lewis and Harris.

8

Cutting peat on the moors, Lewis

In Lewis in particular the crofting system, so stubbornly persistent throughout the Western Highlands and Islands, still retains many of its primitive characteristics, above all its ancient common rights in the township land, and has attracted much intensive study by agricultural economists. The average Lewis croft consists of four or five acres, upon which the principal crops are oats, potatoes and barley; turnips and cabbage are sometimes grown, while some of the crofters have even gone the length of providing themselves with a small garden. The cattle and sheep are pastured on the unenclosed surrounding grass lands. The practice of "summering" by which the cattle are taken to the higher pastures during six weeks or thereby in the warm weather, still continues, though steadily diminishing: and the shielings or huts in which the herdsmen live during the period of "summering" are thatched or turfed afresh each season. In localities where the common pasture round the crofting communities is ample, summer pasturing tends more rapidly to decline. The practice is now restricted to the cattle: the crofters' sheep are allowed to roam at will over the open moorlands all twelve months of the year, though naturally in stormy weather they tend to seek their food upon the lower grounds. In former days sheep were everywhere in Scotland folded at night time, for protection against raiders and wolves.

Much romantic sentiment has gathered around these shielings, and indeed the practice of summering appears to be regarded, at all events by the younger members of the crofting communities, as something of a jaunt. Nearly a century ago a great Highland landlord, of proud and ancient lineage, who understood the economy of his vast estates and the mentality of his tenants as few have ever done, wrote thus upon the topics of "summering" and shielings:[1]

Every one who has walked much among the Highland mountains must have come with surprise, every here and there, upon curious marks of deserted habitations, in very secluded and distant spots . . . Almost anywhere among the hills we may find ourselves among little rings of mouldered wall—or of turfy ridges, sometimes circular, sometimes oblong, always very small, and generally placed in groups—suggesting rather the huts of a temporary encampment than any permanent buildings. They are always above

[1] The Eighth Duke of Argyll, *Scotland as it was and as it is*, 2nd ed. (1887) pp. 198–200.

the steep sides of glens, and they are never on the stony shoulders
of peaks, or upon the summits. Sometimes they are among sudden
knolls where the ground is dry, and where little tracts of soft green
grass are invaded by tufts of heath, and look as if they would soon
be covered by it altogether. Sometimes they are in natural hollows
through which a burn flows, where the dipper flits and dives, and
where the heron watches by the side of little pools. Sometimes they
are on the top of sudden braes rising over a moor loch rich in water
lilies, and lively with surface rings and dimples, which show it to be
populous with trout. But everywhere and always, if we look
around, we can see that those who came there, to live or visit for
a time, had an eye to the best pasture, the best shelter, and access to
a fresh spring or to some running water. These are the summer
"shealings", so famous in Highland history and the poetry of
which makes men as mad now, as it made a primitive population
happy, two hundred years ago. That population went to these
distant and lonely spots for the one sufficient reason that their cattle
would not go to them unless they were taken there, and unless they
were herded by the men and women and children during a few
weeks in the middle of summer . . . The only way of turning to
any human use, even the most favoured bits of the upland pastures,
was for the whole population of the villages or townships to turn
out of their homes, with all their stock, at a certain season of the
year, and migrate to some spot where pasture could be found
sufficiently good, and sufficiently continuous to support for a time
all the cattle and other stock belonging to them. It was always, no
doubt, a delightful time. From the smoky habitations deep in the
hollows, where often the sun shone for a few hours only out of the
twenty-four, it must have been a pleasant and a wholesome change
to live almost wholly in the open air, amongst the fragrant heather,
and with the splendid afterglows of the short midsummer nights
setting off all the hills around in the superbest colouring.

Another primitive agricultural custom which can be studied in
Lewis and Harris, as indeed elsewhere in the Hebrides, is cultivation in "lazy beds". This is mainly in use for the growing of
potatoes, especially where the soil is peaty. A ridge of ground,
about four or six feet wide, and ten in length, is surrounded by
a ditch and then covered with dung, over which is spread the
earth taken out of the ditch. In this the potatoes are planted, with
the aid of a "dibble" or long pointed stick, furnished with a side
pin to act as a combined tread and stop. These "potato mat-
tresses," for so they have been described, form an enduring
feature in the topography of the Hebrides, and may be recognized

on the sites of crofting townships now long extinct. The green patches of the former "lazy beds" are marked out by their lateral ditches, now in their season bright with orchids and other damp-loving flowers.

Some of the coastal crofters eke out an addition to their scanty livelihood by inshore fishing; but the main ancillary occupation of the Lewis and Harris crofters is weaving, in which they have cherished an inherited skill that has made "Harris Tweed" famous throughout the world, and brings much money into the island. A great stability and encouragement was given to this remarkable industry by a decision in 1964 of the Court of Session, which, after a hearing apparently without parallel for sheer length in Scottish legal history—not even excepting the famous case of *Peebles* v. *Plainstanes*!—declared that only cloth made from virgin Scottish wool, dyed, spun and finished in the Outer Hebrides, and hand-woven by the islanders in their own homes, could be sold as "Harris Tweed". Today the yarn is mostly spun and dyed in Stornoway, and sent out to the crofters for weaving. "Hand-weaving" is nowadays a somewhat elastic term, for all the cottage weavers today use imported steel looms, worked by the feet. These looms are usually situated in sheds or annexes adjoining the crofter's house. It is now almost exclusively a man's job. One of the most grateful sounds to be heard as you approach a Lewis croft is the click-clack of the weaver's loom. Recent surveys indicate that the tweed industry is overmanned. It will doubtless be affected by alternative employment offered by the oil industry. There is a project to develop sites at Glamaig Bay and Arnish Point for the maintenance and repair of semi-submersible oil-rigs. There are also plans for building houses and schools in the area. It is estimated that about six million yards of cloth are produced every year, and about 75 per cent of this colossal output is exported, all the world over. Over 5,000 different coloured dyes, or combination of colours, are in use, and constant additions are being made to the varieties of tweed, and to the purposes for which it is used.

East of Stornoway the coast of Lewis runs out into the curious peninsula of Eye, in shape not unlike a crab's claw, and measuring about eight miles in length. Connected with the main island by a narrow sand spit, along the southern edge of which the road is carried on an embankment, the Eye peninsula, which forms a natural breakwater for Stornoway harbour, is mainly composed of Lewisian gneiss; but the area next Stornoway, and the coast line for some miles to the north, is formed of reddish or chocolate-coloured sandstones and conglomerates—the much-discussed Stornoway beds, whose geological horizon has not been ascertained. They appear to be of freshwater origin, laid down under torrential conditions; but, so far, have yielded no fossils. The total thickness of these deposits is not less than 9,000 feet. The Eye peninsula is fertile soil, and is thickly studded with crofting communities, some of whom are part-time fishermen. Its name is derived from Norse *eidh*, an isthmus or neck of land, pronounced in Lewis *aeidh*.

Immediately after crossing the narrow neck of the Eye peninsula, we notice on our left side the ancient church of St Columba, roofless but otherwise more or less entire, and well looked after under the guardianship of the Ministry of Public Building and Works. The church is of two dates, the main portion possibly of the fourteenth century, with a westward extension added perhaps about 1500. The architectural details are of no special distinction. Within the church, however, are preserved two medieval tomb-stones of considerable importance. One displays, in bold relief, the figure of a Hebridean warrior in the familiar panoply of quilted hacketon, pointed basinet, and chainwork camail. Though the head is frontal, the figure stands sideways, as if advancing to the left. His left hand grasps the hilt of his sword and in his right he holds a spear. The carving is superior to the usual run of such monuments. Since Eye Church was the burial place of the Macleods of Lewis, no doubt the figure represents a chieftain of that clan. It is said to be that of Roderick, the seventh chief, who ruled in the time of James IV.

The other grave-slab shows foliaceous and animal devices with a fine cross-pattern of interlaced work at the head. An inscription, no longer legible, bears that the stone commemorates Margaret, daughter of Roderick Macleod of Lewis, and wife of Lachlan MacKinnon, and records her death in 1503. She was the mother of the last Abbot of Iona. On the floor of the church is another slab displaying a claymore.

In general, the surface of Lewis presents the aspect of a rolling, hummocky, spacious moorland, at few places attaining a height of more than 300 feet. Of the 683 square miles of the island, something less than 3 per cent is arable. The rest is grass-land or peat.

Much of it is water-logged, and there are large areas of sedge and cotton grass. Whiter than the cotton grass was the breast of the high-bosomed daughter of Rurmar: and certainly on these broad empty moorlands, drab and desert as they are, we sense the full melancholy of an Ossianic landscape. A feature of the widespread scene is the extraordinary number of lochans and tarns, many of them bright with water lilies in the early summer. On the few hills, which nowhere reach 2,000 feet, coarse heath is found. The climate is mild, and the average rainfall about 50 inches per annum. The coast is rocky, sometimes rising into steep though not very lofty cliffs, but including, particularly on the western side, sandy bays and broad grassy stretches of *machair*, often gay with red and white clover, purple orchids, primroses, and modest daisies and meadow-sweet. The Forestry Commission have a small plantation at Roag. On this side deep fiords are found, notably East and West Lochs Roag, which with their rocky flanks and numerous islets, remind one much, though on a reduced scale, of the Rogaland coast of Norway.

The extreme western promontory of Lewis is indented by the noble bay of Uig, a fine crescent of glistening white sand backed by green dunes and bluff braes, behind which the rocky hills are cleft by Loch Suinaval, long and narrow, and the deepest fresh-water loch in Lewis, with a maximum depth of over 200 feet. Over all in the background rises the highest mountains in Lewis, Mealisval (1,885 feet). The next highest, in the south-eastern corner of Lewis, is Ben More (1,874 feet).

In 1831 a cow, rubbing herself against a sand hill on the southern arc of Uig Bay, dislodged a remarkable hoard of articles made out of walrus ivory, including fourteen draughtsmen and seventy-eight chess pieces. Eleven of these chessmen are preserved in the National Museum of Antiquities of Scotland; the remainder, along with all the draughtsmen, unfortunately found their way into the British Museum. The costume of the chessmen indicates that they were made in the twelfth century. Apparently the site had been occupied by a hut circle.

A feature of the Lewisian scene that will strike every visitor is the "skinned lands". On these the peat has been successively removed, layer by layer, until the underlying stony drift of tawny clay has been bared. Bleached white by the acids of the overlying peat, the stones lend an added ghastliness to the general aspect of desolation.

Stornoway of course is the centre of the road system of Lewis. To the north, a good road extends by Newmarket as far as Tolsta. A mile beyond the town another road, branching to the north-west, crosses the island to Barvas, where it forks, the right hand branch continuing northward along the coast to Port of Ness near the Butt of Lewis, from which continuations lead north-west to Eoropie and south-east to Skigersta. From Barvas the other branch holds south-westward along or near the coast to Carloway, whence southward round the heads of East and West Lochs Roag to Uig. Cross-roads connect Loch Roag with Stornoway. The main road southward from the island capital runs through the superb mountain scenery of Harris, down to Tarbert, skirting round the heads of Loch Erisort and Loch Seaforth. By these main roads, and by various branches connected therewith, most parts of Lewis can be visited comfortably with a car: but he who wishes really to see the island, with all its scenic variety, its flora and fauna, its antiquarian interest, and its opportunities for varied recreation, must be fit and willing to use "Shank's Mare".

Lewis is an angler's paradise. Many of its countless lochs have been stocked with brown trout; sea trout and salmon may be caught in the rivers and estuaries, and the Minch offers superb facilities for open sea fishing. There is never any difficulty about hiring a boat and handlines. Good sea bathing may be enjoyed on fine beaches within easy reach of Stornoway. Of these the best is perhaps Traigh Mhor, north of Tolsta Head. This is a splendid reach of gleaming white sand, a mile and a half in length. But all round the island the visitor will come across unexpected charming sequestered sandy coves. Another kind of recreation for which the island offers unrivalled opportunities is bird-watching. In the policies of Lews Castle is found the only rookery in the Outer Hebrides. Among the numerous birds to be noted here, recent arrivals are the collared dove and the blue tit. Starlings have multiplied so as to form a serious nuisance to the crofters. Along the shores, on cliff and beach, a vast variety of seafowl can be spotted. Mention may be made of the colonies of kittiwakes and fulmar petrels at Tiumpan Head, the extreme point of the Eye peninsula; and the large ternery at Melbost, on the north side of the narrow neck of the same peninsula. Both for native and for migrant species, the environs of Stornoway must be accounted among the most promising fields of ornithological study in Britain.

Within the compass of this modest volume it would be idle to attempt a description, even an inventory, of the antiquities of Lewis. Burial cairns, standing stones and circles and settings of stones, *duns* and brochs, and Celtic and early medieval churches are here to be examined, provided the student has thick boots and a stout walking stick—and also, be it added, a water-proof waterproof, or, better still, an oilskin. Here I shall, therefore, limit myself to a short note about three major monuments: the famous stone circle at Callanish: the broch of Carloway, and the early medieval church at Eoropie.

Of all the stone circles in Britain, none save Stonehenge itself exceeds in weird impressiveness the Standing Stones of Callanish, on a desolate moorland overlooking the head of Loch Roag. Here we find a circle 37 feet in diameter, consisting of thirteen tall pillars, grey and hoary with lichen. This is approached from the north by an avenue of pillars, 27 feet wide, extending for a length of 270 feet and now containing nineteen stones. To the south the avenue is continued, but shorter now and reduced in width; there remain here only six stones. On either side of the circle extends a "cross-arm", composed in each case of four stones. Within the circle is a chambered cairn, which was found to contain a cremated burial: and at the west side of this, opposite the entrance to the chamber, rises the tallest pillar of all, 15 feet 7 inches in height above present ground level.

It is impossible not to think of this great megalithic complex save in terms of ritual. We imagine the chambered cairn as the burial place of a priest-king, and the stone circle, with its stately avenue of approach, as erected afterwards to serve the purpose of ancestor worship by his successors. But what sort of ritual did they carry out in so impressive a temple? We shall never know. We can do no more than echo the lament of Ossian: "Where are our chiefs of old? Where our kings of mighty name? The fields of their battles are silent. Scarce their mossy tombs remain."[1]

The visitor to Callanish should not fail to inspect, in the crofting township hard by the stone circle, one of the best preserved examples of a "black house". Close beside it a "white house" points the contrast.

A few miles north of Callanish is Dun Carloway, one of the finest brochs in Scotland. Grandly crowning a rocky peninsula

[1] For a fuller discussion of Callanish reference may be made to my book, *The Ancient Stones of Scotland* (1965), pp. 62–3.

rising about 150 feet above the south shore of Loch Carloway, the ruined tower is preserved, at one point, to a height of no less than 30 feet, and far and near forms a dominating feature of the scene. The broch, which is 47 feet in diameter, presents the usual characteristic of an entrance door with guard chamber; mural galleries; and a stair winding round the tower. The broch has been carefully repaired, and is maintained as an ancient monument by the Ministry of Public Building and Works.

At Eoropie near the Butt of Lewis, the northmost point of the island (where there is a high-perched red-brick lighthouse, whose beam is visible for 17 miles) stands the remarkable early church known as Teampull Mholuidh, St Moluag's Church. Long a roofless ruin, it was restored in 1912, and is used for an occasional service by the Scottish Episcopal Church. Large by insular standards, the church measures 44 feet by 17 feet 8 inches within the walls. Unicameral so far as the absence of a stone division between nave and chancel is concerned, it possesses two transepts, or rather transeptal chapels (since they are walled off from the chancel) so placed that their east ends are flush with the east gable of the church. As far as preserved, the doors and windows are round-arched, but the east gable window has a pointed rear-arch. The plan, with its small side chapels placed at or very near the eastern end, is an early Norse one, typical of the twelfth and thirteenth centuries. It is found, for example, in the twelfth century Norse Cathedral at Gardar (Igaliko) in Greenland; and the Danish archaeologist who excavated the latter, and who compared its plan with that of our church at Eoropie, considers that the disposition of the chapel wings is the result of Cistercian influence. He points out its close resemblance to the plan of the earliest Cistercian Abbey church in Norway, Lyse Kloster near Bergen, founded in 1146. Another twelfth century feature at Eoropie is the putlog holes in the walls, used for the scaffolding during the course of erection. There can be no doubt that in Teampull Mholuidh we must recognize a church founded or re-established on a Celtic site about the end of the twelfth century, under the patronage of some Norse or Celto-Norse chief in the Lews. Clearly the building was of exceptional importance. It possessed a famous sanctuary, and perhaps it is not without significance that in local tradition it is styled "the Cathedral".

St Moluag, to whom this church is dedicated, was one of the great Irish missionaries who carried the Gospel far and wide among the Picts of Alba. "Moluag, the pure and brilliant, the gracious and decorous", as his disciples loved to call him, was a contemporary of St Columba, though he appears to have worked quite independently of Iona. Establishing a base of operations on the green and lovely island of Lismore, Moluag thence extended his missionary journeys throughout eastern and northern Pictland as far east as Clova in the uplands of Kildrummy and Clatt in the Garioch, as far north as the Butt of Lewis on the west and Rosemarkie on the east, at which latter place he died on 25th June, 592.

It is a well known fact that early Christian church sites are often found to adjoin, or even occupy, the stone circles of pagan times. This was in accordance with the advice given by Gregory the Great to Mellitus, the first Saxon Bishop of London, whom he recommended not to destroy the heathen temples, but to convert them into churches, "so that the people may, forsaking their error, be moved the more oft to haunt their wonted places to the honour and service of God". This may have been the reason why the missionaries from Lismore chose to plant an important church at the extreme north end of the Long Isle: for Eoropie was the scene of a remarkable heathen cult, the worship of a sea-god called "Shony", of whom nothing appears to be known elsewhere; and whose worship at Eoropie, despite St Moluag and all that the Christian Church could do, survived until the seventeenth century, when it was finally abolished through the persistent efforts of Presbyterianism. The curious thing is that the cult of this pagan deity was actually conducted within Teampull Mholuidh.

The traveller Martin Martin has preserved for us a detailed account of the observance, which took place on All Hallows Day. On that day the inhabitants of Lewis, coming from far and near, assembled at Eoropie. Each family group brought a peck of malt, which they brewed into ale. Then one of the company was chosen to wade out at night into the sea, carrying a cup of ale. When the water had reached his waist he stood still, and in a loud voice cried out to the sea-god, saying: "Shony, I give you this cup of ale, hoping you'll be so kind as to send us plenty of seaware for enriching the ground for the ensuing year." Having finished this prayer, he cast the cup of ale into the sea. Thereafter the entire company entered the church, upon the altar of which had been placed a lighted candle. Before this the worshippers remained a while in silence. Then, upon a signal from the leader, the light was quenched, and the company went forth into the fields, where they spent the rest of the night drinking their ale, amid singing and dancing. Upon the punctual observance of their "solemn anniversary", as it was called by Martin, the islanders firmly believed that their supply of sea-ware depended for the ensuing twelve months.

The worship of St Moluag himself was attended by many superstitious observances at Eoropie. In particular, the Saint was held to be a sovereign healer of wounds. People who had sustained a limb injury would bring or send a wooden replica of the afflicted member to the church to be laid upon the altar, invoking St Moluag to effect a cure. A visitor in 1630 says that he saw several wooden limbs lying there. Lunatics were also brought to Teampull Mholuidh, and were said to have been restored to their senses within the church.

One of the earliest descriptions of Lewis is found in a curious story told in the *Chronicle of Man*. We there read how, about the year 1208, Reginald, King of Man,

> gave to his brother Olaf a certain island that is called Lewis. It is said to be more extensive than the other islands, but it is cultivated by few inhabitants, because it is mountainous and rocky, and almost wholly inarable. Its inhabitants live principally by hunting and fishing.
>
> Therefore Olaf set out to take possession of this island; and dwelt in it, leading a sorry life. And when he saw that it was by no means sufficient for his own support, and that of his army, he went confidently to his brother Reginald, who then abode in the islands, and spoke to him thus: "Brother", said he, "and my lord King, thou knowest that the Kingdom of the Islands pertained to me by hereditary right. But since the Lord has chosen thee to govern it, I do not grudge it thee, or bear it ill that thou art raised up in royal eminence. Now therefore I beg thee to provide me with some portion of land in the islands, in which I can honourably live with my followers; because the island of Lewis which thou gavest me is unable to support me."

Brother Reginald's reply to this petition was to clap the wretched Olaf in chains and to hand him over to William the Lion, by whom he was kept in durance vile for nearly seven years. When in 1214 Alexander II succeeded to the Scottish throne he released the captive, who made his way to Man, and after a pilgrimage to the great shrine of St James at Compostella, was restored by his brother to his lordship in Lewis. Those who care may follow in the *Chronicle of Man* his subsequent vivid and violent career, until the Manxmen, turning against King Reginald, summoned Olaf to mount his throne.

Before we leave Lewis a word must be said about the religious climate of the island. At the Disruption in 1843 the majority of the islanders "came out" with the Free Kirk. Since then they have been marked, in general, by the extremest form of Calvinism. Even in Stornoway, in its own small way a cosmopolitan community, many of whose inhabitants are not of Gaelic race, but incomers from the Lowlands, Sabbatarianism assumes forms which the visitor, however much he will respect the sincerity of its devotees, is bound to feel oppressive. Music, dancing, drinking and conviviality, those ancient Highland amusements, are frowned upon, sometimes fiercely denounced from the pulpit. Village halls, so greatly needed for the social welfare and education of the crofting townships, have encountered much clerical opposition, which (with one or two honourable exceptions) has extended itself even to the "University Weeks" promoted by the education authority with the co-operation of the University of Aberdeen. "All we can offer to our parishioners", observed a Lewis minister in rejecting a lecture on the Dead Sea Scrolls, "is the simple word of God, and we do not wish them to have anything else." Among the stricter sort, all Sunday work, even cooking, is forbidden. The wireless sets are silent. Travel, except in cases of dire necessity, was long regarded as sinful—though it is right to say that it is now increasingly used for Sunday services. The fishermen must reach port by midnight on Saturday, and dare not set forth again before midnight on Sunday. The theology expounded from the island pulpits may seem too often to draw its inspiration from the sterner passages of the Old Testament, rather than from the Gospel proclaimed by the compassionate Redeemer of Mankind. Yet all this extreme puritanical rigidity is slowly yielding—due partly to the fact that the younger folk are no longer prepared to submit to it, and partly to the experience of a wider world which so many Lewismen have gained through service in two World Wars. Lastly and by no means least, divinity students from the Hebrides who might be expected, after completing their course at university and training college, to return

to their native isles and there put their knowledge of Gaelic to
effect, have too often preferred to seek a mainland charge where
the religious atmosphere is less stifling. Thus the care of the insular
churches tended to fall more and more into the hands of semi-
educated crofters, with the inevitable result of a decline in the
prestige of the ministry.

The emancipation from clerical tyranny, now in progress
among the younger folk in Lewis, carries along with itself its own
peculiar dangers. In their revulsion from the distorted and
narrow version of Christianity too often presented to them,
too many are tempted to turn their backs upon the Christian
faith itself. Samuel Johnson, reflecting upon Scottish Presbyterianism almost two centuries ago, sagely remarked that the
old "sullen scrupulousness" was "now visibly abating, and
giving way too fast to their laxity of practice and indifference
of opinion, in which men, not sufficiently instructed to find the
middle point, too easily shelter themselves from rigour and
constraint."

Harris

The traveller who drives his car from Stornoway along the
35 miles of road down to Tarbert will be astonished at the abrupt-
ness of the change between the open, rolling, hummocky, water-
logged and tarn-dotted uplands of Lewis and the steep rocky
light-grey mountains, with their screes and corries, that make up
the Deer Forest of Harris. The contrast is all the more surprising
when we reflect that the geological materials of both "islands"
are mostly the same—Lewisian gneiss. Faulting and uplift, occurring at a very early period, have produced the Harris mountains,
though their present contours are due to intense glaciation and
long-continued frost. Mostly the summits, where not indeed
rock, are clothed with grass: what little heather there is tends to
be stunted. The highest summit, the great granitic mass of The
Clisham (2,622 feet) affords good rock climbing, not to be under-
taken without a skilled guide. The coast is rocky, with numerous
small beaches, often strewn with shell sand. It is much indented
with fiords, which in their present form are drowned valleys,
though it has been suggested that some of them originated in
"tension clefts". Recent submergence is attested by stretches of
peat occurring now even under low-water mark.

Of all the Harris fiords, the finest is Loch Seaforth, which separates it from Lewis. Eighteen miles in length, and 54 fathoms in greatest depth, it forks at its upper end round Seaforth Island. From it the Mackenzies of Kintail, owners of Lewis from 1611 until their forfeiture after the Fifteen, took the title of their Earldom, since the country round the head of Loch Seaforth was their favourite hunting ground. To the famous Highland Regiment which they raised in 1778 they gave the name of their peerage, so that the renown of this sequestered Hebridean loch has been carried all round the world in many a stirring deed of arms—until the identity of this proud regiment was submerged by an unimaginative War Office.

Another fine Harris fiord is Loch Shell (Sealg), on the east coast north of Loch Seaforth. Near its head, at Eisken Lodge, the visitor is surprised, in this desolate landscape, to come upon a fine garden enclosed by stately trees, including Spanish chestnuts, copper beeches, sycamore, ashes and pines.

Harris forms a renowned deer forest; and here also grouse and mountain hare may be shot, as well as geese and pigeons on the low grounds. The freshwater lochs of Harris offer superb angling facilities, and the sea fishing is as good as any in the Outer Isles. Apart from catering for sportsmen and tourists, crofting and fishing, as in Lewis, are the mainstay of the population, which today, alas! does not much exceed 3,500. The Isle of Harris now enjoys its own electricity, generated by a dam and power plant on Loch Chliostair. This little lake is close to Amhuinnsuidhe Castle, a handsome edifice erected in the last century by the Earl of Dunmore. Here Sir James Barrie wrote the first draft of *Mary Rose*. The tweeds which have made the name of Harris so famous are woven here equally as in Lewis, and under the same general conditions of organization and economics. Equally renowned is Harris knitwear, produced by many of the crofters' womenfolk.

Like Lewis, Harris is an irresistible magnet for the bird watcher. Its mountain fastnesses are the refuge of the golden eagle, the buzzard, and the falcon, while on the rocky coastline guillemots, shags, fulmars, and many other seabirds nest in their countless thousands. Standing stones, cairns, *duns*, hut circles, and ruined churches form an equal attraction to the antiquary: in a category by itself is Rodil Church, to be noted later.

At Northton, on the low western shore of Harris, amid an

extensive range of sand-dunes, a prehistoric site of prime importance was discovered in 1964 by Professor James S. McEwen, of
the Chair of Church History in the University of Aberdeen. It is
now being excavated by Mr Derek Simpson, of the University of
Leicester: and, by the kind permission of both, I am privileged
to present my readers with the following brief provisional sum-
mary of the results achieved up to date.

The earliest period of occupation dates from a time when no
more than a couple of feet of wind-blown sand had accumulated
upon the old land surface of glacial till. The pottery recovered is
of Neolithic character, and closely resembles that manufactured
in the famous kiln-site at Eilean an Tighe, North Uist, to be noted
later (see page 144). The midden refuse associated with these
potsherds included sea-shells and bones of cattle, sheep, deer and
birds. Tools were made of bone and antler, and included two
small combs. In a roughly oval boulder-grave was found the
crouched burial of a child.

Above this layer of primary occupation, and separated from it
by about a foot of blown sand, was a second midden, its soil
reddened with peat ash. Here again there were limpets, dog-
whelks and cockles, and bones of animals wild and domestic,
many marked with knife cuts. A stone-built house was partly
uncovered: it appeared to be semi-subterranean, scooped and
revetted in the sand. Stake holes indicated that this hut had some
kind of a wooden roof. The dwelling had a stone hearth. Scattered over the floor were numerous animal bones, including
whale, tools of bone and antler, flint and quartz, and quantities
of Beaker pottery—but including also some sherds of a Food
Vessel of Irish type. This then, must be one of the earliest habitations so far recorded from the Outer Hebrides.

Ultimately the little settlement appears to have been over-
whelmed by sand; but above this there were, so far as research has
meantime revealed, at least two subsequent occupations by the
Beaker folk. Altogether this must be accounted a highly complex
and deeply interesting site; and as it is in danger of being carried
away by the sea, it is a matter of national importance that means
should be forthcoming to complete the work.

After winding through the magnificent scenery of North Harris,
alternately climbing and dipping down in breath-taking fashion,
the road finally descends to the isthmus of Tarbert, less than a
mile in width, a low sandy spit between East and West Lochs

Tarbert. East Loch Tarbert forms a capacious and sheltered anchorage, and is the port of Harris, as well as a notable centre of white fishing. Here MacBrayne's motor vessel, with a car ferry accommodating 50 vehicles, calls two or three times every day (except Sunday) from Uig in Skye. The vessel can carry a large number of passengers and is equipped with stabilizers and every modern luxury. The voyage from Uig takes about a couple of hours. Tarbert is a most attractive place. It has a good hotel, standing in its own grounds; while many of the neat white houses cater for summer visitors. In its sheltered hollow, Tarbert can boast some respectable clumps of trees, and every newcomer to the place will be struck with the tidiness and brightness of the little gardens—by no means a characteristic of the Hebrides. Tarbert is the shopping centre for Harris, and, despite its scattered lay-out, has quite the aspect of a miniature capital. The only industry is a carding mill. A village hall and a playing field are the legacy of Leverhulme.

From Tarbert a second-class road runs southward along the east coast, then traverses South Harris through Glen Laxdale, and continues down the west coast until, at a distance of 27 miles from Tarbert, it terminates at Rodil, where there is a hotel. This is the road that the traveller should follow if he wishes to see the country. If, on the other hand, he is pressed for time to inspect the famous Church of Rodil, a fairly good road will conduct him from the *col* above Glen Laxdale down the east coast, winding round the heads of innumerable sea lochs, and passing through Geocrab and Finsbay.

Going by Laxdale, the traveller will notice a number of small cairns upon either side of the road. These have been placed to mark the stages at which coffins rested as they were borne on the mourners' shoulders to the large cemetery at Luskentyre, on the north side of the Laxdale estuary. Coming round this way, the visitor will have the opportunity of seeing Borve Lodge, Viscount Leverhulme's Harris seat. Despite its many "outshots" the house is of modest size, containing no more than seven bedrooms. A feature of the grounds is the circular walled garden. Further south is Leverburgh, formerly Obbe. Here, as we have already noted, Viscount Leverhulme in the last stages of his activity began to establish a fishing harbour. His piers for landing herring, and one or two of his installations and dwelling houses still remain, as well as his road to Finsbay on the east coast: but his community centre,

Stone circle at Callanish, Lewis
Vast moors near Stornoway, Lewis
Tarbert, Harris

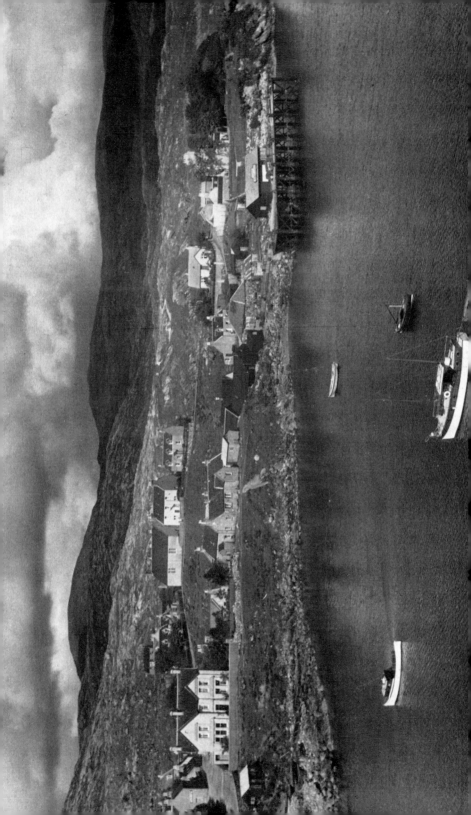

Hulme Hall, is now a school. At the height of his activity in Lever-burgh he brought in some smart English typists from Port Sun-light. These luckless girls aroused the wrath of a local preacher, who from his pulpit declaimed against "the harlots and concu-bines of Lever running about the streets of Obbe!"

At Stockinish, six miles south of Tarbert, on the east side, is the first Youth Hostel in the Long Island, opened on 1st June, 1965. It has 30 beds and cooking facilities, and there is a resident warden. Here also there is a large lobster pond.

St Clement's Church, Rodil, is by far the most remarkable ecclesiastical building in the Outer Isles. The church was built by Alasdair Crotach, eighth chief of the Clan Macleod (1498–1547) and contains his sumptuous altar tomb, designed as an integral part of the structure. Founded upon a rocky site, amid extremely picturesque surroundings, the church is cruciform, consisting of an embattled tower, a nave without aisles, transepts, and a chancel. Internally the building, excluding the tower, measures 61 feet in length. The tower stands on the summit of the rock, and from its interior, a flight of steps in the south and east walls leads down into the nave. There is no structural division between nave and chancel; but the transepts open through pointed arches, richly moulded. The east window is of three trefoiled lights, with wheel tracery in the pointed head. A feature of all departments of the building is its profusion of ornament, in a style which leaves us in little doubt that the mason-craftsmen came from Iona. Most of the dressed work is in green Triassic sandstone from Carsaig in Mull. That this imported material had to be used sparingly is shown by the fact that while it was used for the south transept arch, the northern arch, and the three mailed effigies, are carved in the local dark hornblende gneiss. Sacred, secular and heraldic adornment reach their climax on the founder's tomb, which bears an ungrammatical Latin inscription recording that he built it in 1528. While other figures in the sculpturing display warriors clad in the typical Hebridean quilted coat, camail and pointed bascinet, the founder himself is shown in complete plate armour, except for a camail. It is, more or less, the type of armour seen on the Black Prince's tomb at Canterbury. One must assume that such an outfit would be rare enough in the Hebrides, and will have descended to Alasdair Crotach from his fourteenth-century ancestors. Two other effigies, presumably of Macleods, are pre-served in the church. One is in plate and the other in the usual

9

Lazybeds on Harris
A croft near Tarbert, Harris
Sands on west coast of South Harris

insular panoply. There are also four of the usual foliaceous slabs and a small free-standing cross, portraying the Crucifixion.

Formerly the hereditary standard bearers of the Dunvegan chiefs, to whom was committed the custody of the Fairy Flag, had their burial place in the chancel of Rodil Church. This tomb, or stone coffin, was provided with an iron grating, about a foot or more beneath the cover stone, and on this grating the body of each dead standard bearer was laid. On every occasion when a standard bearer was buried, "the coffin was opened, and all that remained of the last who had been buried in it was shaken down through the bars of the grating into the bottom of the coffin, and the body of the new occupant was laid in it. In this way the ashes of successive standard bearers mingled in one coffin." The family historian who relates this weird tale tells us how his grandfather, early in the eighteenth century, had been present at the funeral of the last hereditary standard bearer, and "saw all the old cere- monies duly performed".

Rodil Church is further believed to hold all that is mortal of Mary Macleod, the famous seventeenth century Gaelic poetess, who was fostered at Uilinish in Skye, but spent most of her life in the household of the Macleods of Bernera.

Rodil Church was restored in 1787, and again very carefully in 1873 by the Countess Dunmore. It is now maintained as a national monument by the Ministry of Public Building and Works. The parsonage of Rodil was impropriated to Holyrood Abbey, and it is possible that the richness of the building may have owed something to the generosity of its distant but wealthy patrons.

Most visitors to the Outer Hebrides make their way thither in summer. To few is it given to witness one of these terrific winter storms, accompanied often by thunder, which burst upon the iron-bound western coasts of the Long Island. Here is a descrip- tion of one such storm, written down more than a century ago by a famous and eloquent naturalist, in the days when men of science were not ashamed to write literature:[1]

Let any one, who wishes to have some conception of the sublime, station himself upon a headland of the west coast of Harris during the violence of a winter tempest, and he will obtain it. The blast howls among the grim and desolate rocks around him. Black clouds

[1] Prof. W. Macgillivray in *Edinburgh Journal of Natural and Geographical Science*, 1830.

are seen advancing from the west in fearful masses, pouring forth torrents of rain and hail. A sudden flash illuminates the gloom, and is followed by the deafening roar of the thunder, which gradually becomes fainter until the roar of the waves upon the shore prevails over it. Meantime, far as the eye can reach, the ocean boils and heaves, presenting one wide-extended field of foam, the spray from the summits of the billows sweeping along its surface like drifted snow. No sign of life is to be seen, save when a gull, labouring hard to bear itself up against the blast, hovers over head, or shoots athwart the gloom like a meteor. Long ranges of giant waves rush in succession towards the shores. The thunder of the shock echoes among the crevices and caves; the spray mounts along the face of the cliffs to an astonishing height; the rocks shake to their summit, and the baffled wave rolls back to meet its advancing successor. If one at this season ventures by some slippery path to peep into the haunts of the cormorant and rock pigeon, he finds them sitting huddled together in melancholy silence. For whole days and nights they are sometimes doomed to feel the gnawings of hunger, unable to make way against the storm; and often during the winter they can only make a short daily excursion in quest of a precarious morsel of food. In the mean time the natives are snugly seated around their blazing peat-fires, amusing themselves with the tales and songs of other years, and enjoying the domestic harmony which no people can enjoy with less interruption than the Hebridean Celts.

This seems to be a convenient place for offering some brief observations upon the racial composition of the Outer Islesmen, and upon the peculiarities of the clan system as manifested among them. While the population is mainly Celtic, it is beyond doubt that the long centuries of Scandinavian colonization and dominance have left their mark upon the people. Thus in Lewis it is claimed that 80 per cent of the place names are Norse in derivation; while a writer of more than a century ago observed that "the islanders of the northern part of Lewis, with their long matted and uncombed hair, which has never been restrained by hat or bonnet from flowing as freely in the wind as their ponies' manes, form perfect living portraits of the ancient Norsemen." This view obtained independent confirmation from the great Danish archaeologist, Worsaae, who visited the Hebrides in 1846. Here is how he has recorded his impressions:[1]

[1] *An Account of the Danes and Norwegians in England, Scotland, and Ireland.* (1852) pp. 268–9.

Throughout Harris and Lewis the Gaelic inhabitants are small, dark-haired, and in general very ugly. But no sooner do we arrive at Ness, than we meet with people of an entirely different appearance. Both the men and women have in general lighter hair, taller figures, and far handsomer features. I visited several of their cabins, and found myself surrounded by physiognomies so Norwegian, that I could have fancied myself in Scandinavia itself, if the Gaelic language now spoken by the people, and their wretched dwellings, had not reminded me that I was in one of those poor districts in the northwest of Europe where the Gaels or Celts are still allowed a scanty existence. . . . It is but a little while ago that the inhabitants of the Naze, who are said to have preserved faint traces of their origin from Lochlin (called also in Ireland, Lochlan), or the North, regarded themselves as being of better descent than their neighbours the Gaels. The descendants of Norwegians seldom or never contracted marriage with natives of a more southern part of the island, but formed among themselves a separate community, distinguished even by a peculiar costume, entirely different from the Highland Scotch dress. Although the inhabitants of Ness are now, for the most part, clothed like the rest of the people of Lewis, I was fortunate enough to see the dress of an old man of that district, which had been preserved as a curiosity. It was of thick coarse woollen stuff, of a brown colour, and consisted of a close-fitting jacket, sewn in one piece, with a pair of short trousers, reaching only a little below the knees.

In later times, Clan Macleod was dominant both in Lewis and in Harris, but in two separate branches. The *Siol Torquil*, descendants of Torquil, held sway in Lewis, while the *Siol Tormod*, ruled over Harris and the Macleod lands in Skye, with their chief seat at Dunvegan Castle. Torquil and Tormod were sons of Leod, the eponymous ancestor of Clan Macleod. But whereas the Dunvegan Macleods continued to hold Harris until 1779, the Lewis branch went down before the royal power of James VI, who in 1598 introduced the celebrated "Fife Adventurers" to bring "civility" to the island, and, upon the collapse of these immigrants in face of insular hostility, handed over Lewis in 1611 to Mackenzie of Kintail, whose family retained it, latterly as Earls of Seaforth, with a short interval of forfeiture after the "Fifteen", until they sold it to Sir James Matheson in 1844. No doubt the Fife Adventurers, and the Fishing Corporation established at Stornoway by Charles I, will have introduced a certain amount of Lowland blood, while the Mackenzie period undoubtedly resulted in some fresh Gaelic settlement from the opposite mainland. Whatever the reasons, alike in their physical type, their mental characteristics, and their Gaelic speech the Lewismen differ somewhat from their neighbours in Harris. Quite apart from having enjoyed a more continuous clan history, the men of Harris must naturally have retained, within their mountain fastnesses, a greater proportion of more ancient racial strains. Indeed it is asserted that the population of Harris includes a recognizable admixture of dark-featured folk, thought to denote the survival of a remote and primitive stock.

It is of course absurd to claim, as sentimentalists are prone to do, that Macleods or Macdonalds or Macneils in the Hebrides, or for that matter all the wide world over, are "members of one family". The truth about the alleged kinship of the clans was plainly set forth, two centuries ago, by James Macpherson in a pithy note to his *Ossian*. In this same remarkable gloss he explains a contrast which must strike everyone who knows the islanders: their deep sense of equality among themselves, particularly in the social and economic relations of their townships, but their instinctive reverence for the Chief or Laird—a reverence, be it added, quite untinged by servility. Here is what Macpherson writes:

> It is a vulgar error that the common Highlanders lived in abject slavery under their chiefs. Their high ideas of, and attachment to the heads of their families probably led the unintelligent into this mistake. When the honour of the tribe was concerned, the commands of the chief were obeyed without restriction: but if individuals were oppressed, they threw themselves into the arms of a neighbouring clan, assumed a new name, and were encouraged and protected. The fear of this desertion no doubt made the chiefs cautious in their government. As their consequence, in the eyes of others, was in proportion to the numbers of their people, they took care to avoid everything that tended to diminish it.

Doubtless owing to the greater continuity of their clan history, I think it possible that the characteristic Celtic combination of reverence for the Chief or Laird and equalitarianism in the township is today more apparent in Harris than in Lewis. Certainly the Harris men gave greater support and loyalty to Viscount Leverhulme than their neighbours in the north. There were no more than a couple of disconnected outbreaks of raiding at Rodil, and the second one was promptly suppressed by the combined action of the islanders. At a meeting with the crofters at Obbe, where Leverhulme spoke to them through an interpreter, the Harrismen pledged full support for their laird in his plans for the island; and, to the day of his death, they kept their word.

No account of the Long Island, however brief, would be complete without some reference to the greatest disaster that has struck its inhabitants in modern times. This was the loss, on New Year's Day, 1919, of H.M.S. *Iolaire* just outside Stornoway harbour. The *Iolaire* was an Admiralty yacht, which was conveying some 260 naval ratings, all natives of the Long Island, back to their homes for their New Year's leave—the first since the beginning of the war, more than four years ago. The night was a wild one, and at 1.55 a.m. the *Iolaire* struck a submerged reef, known ominously as "Beast of Holm", at the entrance to Stornoway Harbour, just opposite Arnish lighthouse. Within a few minutes the ship overturned, and in less than an hour and a half had sunk. So violent was the storm that the only two lifeboats which could be launched were promptly smashed to flinders. When the dawn broke, only the canted masts of the sunken vessel showed above water, and to one of them clung a half-frozen survivor. Of the 260 passengers and crew of 25, no less than 206 were drowned. And this "unspeakable tragedy", as the Chamberlain of the Lews described it in his telegram to Leverhulme, took place within twenty feet of the shore, and hardly a mile from Stornoway harbour, where, despite the weather, a large crowd had assembled to greet their returning war-heroes with a Hogmanay welcome. Scarcely a home in Lewis and Harris was not smitten by bereavement.

All but half a century has elapsed since that fatal night. Yet, even now, the oldest islanders can talk about it only with subdued voices or bated breath.

VII

THE SMALL STRAY ISLETS

About 45 miles northwards from the Butt of Lewis lies the remote island of North Rona, a chunk of hornblende-schist covering some 300 acres, and rising to a maximum height of 355 feet. It is now tenanted only by sheep, ferried across for the grazing season from the Ness of Lewis.

On the southern side of the island, which is roughly triangular in shape, is *Teampull Ronain*, St Ronan's Chapel, a primitive structure of which the oldest part, now the chancel, has walls converging upwards, both outside and inside, and formerly covered by a stone-slabbed roof. In the south wall is a small rude aumbry, little more than a hole. Though later, the nave is of cruder and more irregular construction than the primary chapel. Both divisions of the little church were originally dry-built, but the chancel, or primary chapel, was subsequently pointed inside.

To judge by Irish parallels, this early chapel on North Rona might well be one of the oldest specimens of Celtic church architecture in the Hebrides. Internally it measures no more than 11 feet 6 inches by 7 feet. It could have been a penitential cell, the refuge of a hermit or recluse, such as is mentioned on two occasions in the *Martyrology of Donegal*. Thus:

> Enda of the high piety loved
> In Ara, victory with sweetness,
> A prison of hard narrow stone
> To bring all unto heaven.

and again:

> Molaisi of the Lake loves
> To be in a prison of hard stone
> To have a house of guests for the men of Erin,
> Without refusal, without a particle of churlishness.

In this second extract we have a picture of the austere Celtic hermit shutting himself up in a narrow stone cell, but also providing hospitable quarters for those visitors who were attracted by his sanctity. It is possible that some of the hut formations closely adjoining *Teampull Ronain* may represent dwellings provided for some such purpose.

In the little churchyard, half sunk in the rank coarse grass, are a number of small, rudely hacked-out crosses, devoid of sculpture. On the west side of the churchyard are a half-dozen of very archaic-looking dwellings, much dilapidated but including three "bee-hive" cells.

Dr John MacCulloch, who visited North Rona in 1818, has given us a grim enough picture of the islanders' houses:

> Such is the violence of the wind in this region that not even the solid mass of a highland hut can resist it. The house is therefore excavated in the earth, the wall required for the support of the roof scarcely rising two feet above the surface. The roof itself is but little raised above the level, and is covered with a great weight of turf, above which is the thatch; the whole being surrounded with turf stacks to ward off the gales. The entrance to this subterranean retreat is through a long, dark, narrow and tortuous passage like the gallery of a mine, commencing by an aperture not three feet high and very difficult to find.

It is not surprising that by the middle of the nineteenth century the last regular inhabitant had quitted the island, whereupon the owner, Sir James Matheson of the Lews, offered it to the Government for use as a penitentiary. Whether for humanitarian reasons or on considerations of expense, the offer, although made *gratis*, was declined.

On an isolated stack called Sula Sgeir, about a dozen miles south-west of North Rona, there are the remains of another primitive hermitage, known alternatively as *Teampull Sula Sgeir* or *Tigh Beannaiche*, "the Blessed House." In construction it much resembles the primary building at *Teampull Ronain*, except that the angles are rounded. Looking for all the world like a petrified peat stack, this little cell much resembles the well known oratory at Kilmalkedar in the County Kerry.

In the North Minch, some 21 miles south of Stornoway, but no more than four miles east of the opposite coast of Lewis, lie the Shiant Isles. The group consists of three islets, now uninhabited, and an assemblage of stacks and skerries. Formed of dolerite overlying Upper Liassic shales, the group are obviously associated with Skye, and may therefore be regarded as the outermost and northmost of the Inner Hebrides. As seen from the motor vessel approaching Tarbert or Stornoway, the Shiant Isles make a striking appearance. Sir Archibald Geikie remarks that "these lonely islets, extending in an east and west direction for about three miles, display in great perfection most of the chief characteristics of the Skye sills. They are especially noteworthy for including the thickest intrusive sheet and the noblest columnar cliff in the whole of the Tertiary volcanic series of Britain." Some of the prismatic columns are nine feet in diameter, and may be traced continuously through a height of over 300 feet.

The name Shiant signifies "the hallowed islands"; and the principal member of the group is called *Eilean na cille*, "Isle of the Church". Some foundations still traceable have been thought to be the remains of an early ecclesiastical settlement. The three major islets are famous for their rich sheep and cattle pastures and their brave array of wild flowers; and the whole group are a notable haunt of seafowl. Upon the dispersal of the Leverhulme estates in 1925 the Shiant Isles were purchased by Mr (now Sir) Compton Mackenzie.

On the opposite side of the Long Island, far out in the broad Atlantic, about 21 miles west of Gallan Head, the westmost point of Lewis, lie the Flannain Isles, otherwise picturesquely known as "the Seven Hunters". They have long been uninhabited, save by the lighthouse keepers and a vast concourse of sea-fowl. The islands belong to the Lewisian gneiss. The largest of the group, Eilean Mor, possesses hard by the lighthouse, a tiny dry-built chapel, or hermit's cell, known as *Teampull Beannachadh* (the blessed). It measures no more than 7¾ feet by 5 feet within the walls. The gables are rather neatly built of curved or pointed form, with well-fitted skew stones; the only opening is the door in the west gable, which has inclined jambs in the Irish manner. Also on this island are two dry-built huts or bothies, one of which has a beehive cell adjoining. These huts are known as the Bothies of the Clan Macphail.

In 1901 the Flannain lighthouse was the scene of a cruel tragedy, when three of its four keepers perished in a storm, the exact circumstances never being ascertained; the fourth member of the crew was on shore leave at the time.

In his *Rerum Scoticarum Historia*, published in 1581, George Buchanan gives a short account of the Flannain Islands, which he describes as a sacred hermitage. They are hilly and grass-grown, he tells us, but uninhabited by human beings: nor are there any beasts other than wild sheep; but these have fat instead of flesh, and what flesh there is no one will eat save in the direst distress.

VIII

NORTH UIST, BENBECULA, SOUTH UIST

The three islands dealt with in this section are now linked, by a causeway between the first two and by a bridge connecting Benbecula with its southern neighbour. The group has direct communication with the Scottish mainland by MacBrayne's car-ferry, which during the season calls daily (except Sunday) at Lochmaddy in North Uist. Since the seventeenth century, when it is recorded that 400 sail were based upon the harbour, Lochmaddy has been a considerable port and fishing centre. With an opening less than a couple of miles wide, between Weaver's Point and Rudha-nam-pleac, Lochmaddy extends inward for more than five miles, and is nearly three miles in maximum width. Its labyrinthine shores—said to be 200 miles in length!—are indented by innumerable embayments and creeks, while the broad face of the loch is studded with islands great and small; so that the impression you get on sailing in is that of an inextricable intermingling of land and sea. A powerful lighthouse on Weaver's Point ensures safety of approach. At the entry are three basaltic islets which Celtic fancy has likened to couchant hounds—hence (it is said) the name Lochmaddy, from the Gaelic *madadh*, a dog, fox, or wolf. The scattered little town is well equipped as the capital of its group of three islands. There is a good hotel, a bank, a post office, county buildings, a cottage hospital and the usual shops. The religious allegiance of the inhabitants is expressed in places of worship belonging to three denominations—the Church of Scotland, the Free Church, and the Free Presbyterian Church.

If the day be clear, the visitor to North Uist should begin by climbing Ben Lee (920 feet), south-east of Lochmaddy. From this vantage point he will get a good general view of the green and pleasant island. It measures about 17 miles in length and 12 miles in breadth. Along the east side are innumerable fiords, a magnet for the sea-fisher; but the cultivated land lies towards the west

coast, where there is a considerable scattering of modestly pros-
perous crofts. The main crops are oats and barley. Sea-ware is
used for manure. The population of the island is in the neighbourhood of 1,900. Generally speaking, the interior is water-logged,
peaty brown moorland, with the usual countless lochans and
tarns, the haunt of geese, ducks and whooper swans. About one
tenth of the land surface is reckoned to be covered with water. In
places the peat may be as much as 15 or 20 feet in depth: and in it
are found embalmed the trunks and roots of oak, fir and birch
trees. Upon the west coast long stretches of *machair*, spangled with
varied wild flowers, overlook miles of solitary beach, including
fine stretches of shelly sand. The north-western coast is rocky, but
the cliffs are not of much height. This western coast of North Uist
lies nearest of all the Long Island to America: and the Gulf Stream
has cast upon its sandy shores such transatlantic flotsam as coco-
nuts, bamboo, Sargasso weed, and seeds, beans and shells from the
West Indies. Even a turtle thus once became an involuntary visitor
to North Uist! The highest point of the island is the pyramidal
Bean Eaval (1,138 feet), in the south-east corner. The uplands
support large herds of red deer. North Uist is composed of Lewisian gneiss, with many basaltic intrusions, derived probably from
the Skye volcano.

The island is now encompassed by a reasonably good and level
road, by means of which all its hidden beauties and antiquarian
treasures can be explored in comfort. A transverse road, cutting
across the north-western promontory of the island, was constructed as a relief work during the potato famine of 1846. At
Loch Eport, on the east side, is a spinning mill, used in connexion
with the Harris tweed industry: and at Sponish, north of Lochmaddy, a factory is engaged in the processing of seaweed, which
is used for animal feeding, and also is converted into synthetic
commodities such as toothpaste, bandages and various edible
commodities. This industry is growing, and full of promise, in
the Long Island: there are factories also at Keose in Lewis and at
North Boisdale in South Uist.

The kelp industry—producing an alkali formerly used in the
making of soap and glass—was first started in the Outer Isles
at North Uist in 1735. It rapidly attained prosperity in the middle
decades of the eighteenth century, during which it spread throughout the Hebrides. The seaweed was burned to produce potash and
soda. It is estimated that some 2,000 tons a year was produced in

the Long Island: the price received was £20 a ton, and the wage of kelp-makers averaged a shilling a day. About 24 tons of sea-weed were required to produce a ton of kelp; every 300 tons produced afforded employment to 200 men during June, July and August. North Uist remained the principal focus of the industry: in 1812 the net proceeds in the island exceeded £14,000. Unfortunately this flourishing industry, which brought a substantial measure of prosperity to the crofters and fishing folk, collapsed as a result of a reduction of the duty on Spanish barilla in 1822, and the discovery in the very next year of a means of producing sodium from salt. For some time kelp burning was continued as a source of iodine—a manufacture revived during the First World War. Grievous as was the blow inflicted upon the Hebridean economy by the decline of kelp-making, it must be confessed that the industry had its dark side. The proprietors claimed the kelp as their own, and forced their tenants to work upon it during the three summer months, which ought to have been devoted to their crofts. Moreover the kelp boom resulted in over-population, with disastrous consequences when the industry folded up.

In 1819 Dr John MacCulloch published the following interesting description of kelp manufacture in North Uist:[1]

Driftwood, thrown on the shores by storms, and consisting chiefly of *fucus digitatus* and *saccharinus*, is used to a certain extent when fresh and uninjured, but the greater part is procured by cutting other plants of this tribe at low water. The method of landing the weed after cutting is simple and ingenious. A rope of heath or birch twigs is laid at low water beyond the portion cut, and the ends are brought upon the shore. At high-water, the whole being afloat together, the rope is drawn at each end, and the included material is thus compelled at the retiring tide to settle on the line of high-water mark. The differences in the declivity of the shores therefore, as well as their linear extent, and the greater or less rise of the tide, together with more or less shelter from the prevalent surge, constitute the chief bases of the variations of a kelp estate ... On some estates they [the *fuci*] are cut biennially, on others once in three years, nor does it seem to be ascertained what are the relative advantages or disadvantages of these different practices. The weed is burnt in a copper of stones, a construction which, however rude it may appear, seems fully adequate to the purpose.

Attempts have been made to introduce kilns of a more refined construction, which have failed from the most obvious cause, the expense

[1] *Description of the Western Islands*, vol. I, p. 122.

of fuel necessary for their support; the inventors appearing to have forgotten that the substance in the ordinary mode of treatment formed its own fuel. The number of these fires which during the summer are forever burning along the shores, give an interest and a life to these dreary scenes; recalling to the spectator's mind the activity of society in regions where all other traces of it are nearly invisible. The poet who indulges in visions of the days of old, may imagine the lighting of the war-fires, and fancy that he sees signals which communicated the news of a Danish descent through the warlike clans.

From what has thus far been said, the reader will have gathered that in geological structure, scenic aspect, vegetation and general conditions of animal and human life, North Uist does not differ materially from Lewis and Harris as already described. Where the island stands forth is in the richness and diversity of its antiquities. North Uist is fortunate in that these attracted the attention, so far back as 1897, of a distinguished archaeologist, the late Dr Erskine Beveridge, who in 1911 consecrated to the antiquities of North Uist a sumptuous volume,[1] which still remains the most elaborate such investigation of any one of the Hebrides, and has by no means been superseded by the survey subsequently conducted by the Royal Commission on Ancient Monuments. Since the latter was published in 1928 more attention has been paid to North Uist by archaeologists than, perhaps, to any other island of the Hebrides.

North and South Uist, with Benbecula between them, formed part of the patrimony of Clan Ranald from the thirteenth to the nineteenth century. At first they were held by the Macruari branch of this great family, known sometimes as Clan Donald North (of Sleat and North Uist): but in 1346 they passed to Clan Donald South through the marriage of the Lady Amie MacRuari to John of Islay, the Chief of Clan Donald South. In the hands of the Macdonalds of the Isles they remained until South Uist was sold off at various periods in the early nineteenth century, and North Uist in 1855.

The long centuries of Macdonald ownership have left one ecclesiastical monument of the first importance in North Uist: Teampull na Trionaid, Trinity Church, on the Carinish peninsula at the south-western corner of the island. This is a well-built unicameral structure of stone and lime. It is of unusual size, measuring internally about 61 feet 6 inches by 21 feet 3 inches. The walls are

[1] *North Uist: its Archaeology and Topography* 1911.

faced with regularly coursed rubble work of split boulders, or large pebbles, carefully chosen for their uniform size, laid in horizontal layers maintained throughout the wall-face, and brought to course as required by pinnings, so that the general effect is to give the wall a striated or banded appearance. Now this is a very early type of masonry, seen for example in the thirteenth-century mainland castles of Dunnideer, Balvenie, Red Castle (Lunan Bay), Rothes, Skipness, Castle Roy and Lochindorb. Moreover, the walls are pierced with putlog holes for wooden frames used in the process of construction: and this, as we noted at Eoropie, is a mark of twelfth-century building practice in the Norse areas of Scotland. The only window with architectural characteristics preserved is a lancet that has every appearance of an early date. Now as to the historical record. It is stated by Macvourich that this church was built by Bethog, (or Beatrice) first Prioress of Iona, early in the thirteenth century; and this assertion is supported by a charter of confirmation, issued in 1389 by Godfrey, Lord of Uist, of the Chapel of the Holy Trinity in Uist, along with the lands of Carinish, to the Abbey of Inchaffray, "as granted to them by Cristina the daughter of Alan the true heiress and Reginald called McRory the true lord and patron." Cristina lived about the year 1309, so that plainly the church was in existence then. Like other structures in the Hebrides, it is said to have been built by the famous Lady Amie of the Isles about the year 1390; but doubtless she merely repaired it for the monks of Inchaffray. It is impossible not to recognize in this building a church erected under Norse rule about the year 1200.[1]

A remarkable feature of this deeply interesting and important church is the detached side chapel, Teampull MacVicar, reached by a vaulted passage from the chancel of the main church. This has an extraordinary, and so far as I am aware unique resemblance to the side chapel, Capel Beuno, similarly sited and reached, at the church of Clynnog Fawr in Caernarvonshire. The masonry of Teampull MacVicar is much inferior to that of the parent church.

To medieval times must also be ascribed the island fortalice of Dun Ban on Loch Caravat. Here, as we have already found at Dunvegan, and as we shall find again at Kisimul, we have the archetypal form of Hebridean castle—a ring wall of stone and

---

[1] On the whole subject of Norse building in the Sudereys reference may be made to the Introduction of my book, *The Castle of Bergen and the Bishop's Palace at Kirkwall* (1961).

lime, having a hall or dwelling house on the side farthest from the entrance. Only here, in this modest castellet, no keep or great tower was afterwards added. The hall roof was stone flagged. The curtain wall is over six feet thick, and is inturned so as to form an alcove for the portal or boat entrance, which was secured by a stout drawbar, 8 inches square. An iron ring, long since removed, served for mooring the boat. The lime has been made with cockle and mussel shells.

The prehistoric antiquities of North Uist, though remarkable for their number, correspond in general to those with which we have thus far become familiar in our survey of the Northern Hebrides. They are cairns, stone circles, individual standing stones, duns and brochs. Our present space, and the pattern of this book, allow only for a brief mention of three outstanding sites: the neolithic pottery kilns at Eilean-an-Tighe, and the chambered cairns of Clettraval and Unival. Something must also be said about the "wheel-houses".

Eilean-an-Tighe is a long, narrow, rocky islet on Loch nan Geireann, in the mid-north of the island. Here excavation has revealed what may well be the oldest potter's workshop so far recorded in Western Europe. The pottery is exceedingly good, illustrating a curious fact about Scottish prehistoric earthenware, that the further back in time you go, the better is its quality. The foundations exposed indicated a hut and a couple of pottery kilns; the quantity of potsherds, including wasters, was so great as to make it absolutely certain that the pottery was not produced merely to supply the needs of Uist.

The chambered cairn, or passage grave, at Clettraval, on the western side of our island, was built at a time when there was no peat in the area, but when the island boasted birch copsewood, since charcoal derived from this tree was found in the burial chamber. At present, the remains of the cairn stand in the middle of a peat bog. In the Iron Age a fort was built partly on top of the cairn, and mostly out of its materials. Within the cairn itself, the burial chamber consisted of five compartments, divided by partitions. The cairn material was a pile of rounded boulders, some of them over a hundredweight in bulk. From the chamber were removed burnt human and animal bones, birch charcoal, stone balls and large quantities of Neolithic and Bronze Age pottery. Much of the Neolithic earthenware had been supplied from Eilean-an-Tighe.

Hills looking north-west from Ardhosaig, Harris
St Clement's Church at Rodil, Harris

At Unival, on the west shore of Loch Huna, a small cist adjoined the chamber. This cist was an original feature, and in fact formed the burial place. Careful observation enabled the excavators to recover the ritual procedure followed in successive funerals. The dead were inhumed, accompanied by the usual pottery. After each burial the body was allowed time to decompose. Then the cist was purified with charcoal—perhaps with the idea of driving the now disembodied spirit from the tomb. On each occasion when a further funeral took place, the bones and urns of the last occupant were then taken out and piled against the walls of the chamber.

North Uist is famous for its wheel-houses. Found elsewhere in the Hebrides, as also in the Nordereys and in Caithness (where they are known as "wags"), these Iron Age dwellings—sometimes described as "aisled round houses"—had a bee-skep roof, of stone or divots, with a louvre or smoke vent above a central hearth. They are circular in shape, more or less, and divided by radial partitions, not unlike the cross-section of an orange or grapefruit, but of course not extending right across the dwelling. The side compartments or cells thus formed were lintelled over at a height of 8 to 10 feet above the floor. There was an elaborate drainage system; and in the floors were sunk box-like receptacles or keeping places.

The relics found in these North Uist wheel-houses show that they were fully occupied in the first few centuries of the Christian era. By no stretch of the imagination could the inhabitants be considered as living in a state of barbarian squalor. Awls or bodkins, needles, borers, hammers and spades of whalebone, picks and other implements of hartshorn, whetstones, smoothers, polishers, whorls, pounders, querns of both types, saddle and rotary; pot-lids and strike-a-lights of stone; earthenware crucibles and casting moulds of clay or stone, and iron slag; carding combs used in weaving—all these objects give us a glimpse into the varied occupations of the wheel-house folk. One dwelling contained a furnace. Household pottery was of brown or red ware, ornamented with patterns either incised or applied, and in no wise differs from the Iron Age earthenware found elsewhere in the Hebrides. The wheel-house dwellers also had an occasional bowl of Samian ware, which must have been imported from the Roman Province. In one wheel-house was picked up a coin of the Emperor Constantius II (A.D. 337–361). An elegant triangular

10

Weaving tweed, Harris
A North Uist spinner

perforated whalebone ornament of Celtic fashion, possibly part of a bridle-bit, has an exact parallel in bronze from an Ayrshire lake-dwelling. The wheel-house folk passed the long dark winter nights in gambling with bone dice. In spite of the evidence of a metal industry, few articles of bronze or iron have been found. That the latter material was scarce is shown by the fact that spear points were made of whalebone, or from the leg bones of sheep. A harpoon head was fashioned from the latter material. It is clear that in the Iron Age metal was scarce in the Hebrides; so bone and horn, indeed stone, had to take its place. The inhabitants had necklaces of jet, the beads of which, or perhaps the raw material, must have been imported from Whitby in Yorkshire. Pendants were made of whalebone or hartshorn, finger rings of hartshorn, and the dandies of the community dressed their hair with combs of the same material. On a whalebone knife handle the owner had cut his name in ogham letters—the ancient alphabet of the Celts, found in Ireland, Cornwall, Wales and Scotland. This is the only ogham inscription so far recorded from the Hebrides.

These excavations in North Uist give us the earliest picture, in any detail, of domestic life in the Outer Hebrides. It is clear that the wheel-houses were occupied for a long period. The Samian ware dates from the second century, the Roman coin from the fourth, and the ogham inscription can hardly be earlier than the seventh century.

Benbecula

Connected since 1960 by a causeway with North Uist, the island of Benbecula closely resembles it in geological structure and scenery, except that it possesses no hills of note—and therefore is mightily belaboured by Atlantic gales. It may perhaps be described as oblong in shape, with a greatest length, east to west, of some eight miles. Its general character has been described, once for all, by MacCulloch:

> The sea here is all islands, and the land all lakes. That which is not rock is sand; that which is not mud is bog; that which is not bog is lake; that which is not lake is sea; and the whole is a labyrinth of islands, peninsulas, promontories, bays and channels.

As usual in the Long Island, the best land is on the west, where there are broad stretches of flower-spangled *machair* looking down upon sparkling sandy beaches. The eastern shore is low, rocky, fretted by sea lochs, and fringed by islets. The interior is water-logged moorland, rising to its greatest height in Rueval (409 feet). At Balivanich is the former R.A.F. aerodrome, the importance of which, during the Second World War, led to the connecting of Benbecula with Loch Boisdale in South Uist by a concrete bridge and a good metalled road. At the airport is what may be described as the community centre of the island, with shops and a garage. There is a daily bus service (Sundays excluded) between the airport and Loch Boisdale. The route passes Greagorry, where the island has its only hotel, a good "howff" for anglers. Here also are a post office, bank and shops.

In Benbecula the two faiths that divide the ecclesiastical allegiance of the Long Islanders meet, in proportions about equal: and already one senses a relaxation of tension, for the two communities, Catholic and Calvinist, have learned, in the main, to live together in tolerance and charity.

Benbecula can boast its fair share of the antiquarian remains, prehistoric and medieval, common throughout the Long Island. The only two that call for a brief notice here are Teampull Chaluim Chille, St Columba's Chapel, near the airfield at Balivanich, and Borve Castle, north-west of Greagorry.

Teampull Chaluim Chille is a ruin of high interest. It consists of a nave with very thick walls, a western doorway having sloping jambs in the Celtic manner, and small rectangular windows; and a chancel, obviously a much later addition, with thin walls, very irregularly set out. Hard by is St Columba's Well, close to which is "a small cairn, about 12 feet wide and 3 feet high, composed of stones carried there as votive offerings by people who came to drink of the water".[1]

Borve Castle is one of the major secular buildings surviving from the Middle Ages in the Outer Isles. This massive, gaunt and lonely keep, now a shattered untended ruin, is said to have been built in the fourteenth century by the Lady Amie of the Isles: and indeed it has all the appearance of being a structure of that date. Probably this is the Castle of Vynvaule (?Benbecula) on record in 1373. It has been a tower-house of great size and strength, measuring about 62 feet in length, and at least 37 feet in breadth. The walls are 9 feet thick. As often in early towers, the interior, three storeys in height, does not seem to have been vaulted: but

[1] *Royal Commission on Ancient Monuments, The Outer Hebrides, Skye and the Small Isles*, p. 99.

the random rubble, set in thick mortar, is not of very early character. Borve Castle seems to have been still occupied in 1625.

Near Borve Castle is the fine bathing beach of Culla Bay, with
a car park.

Benbecula, indeed the Long Island generally, is forever
associated with the wanderings of the fugitive Prince Charles
Edward. After crossing the Minch in "a stout eight-oared boat",
amid "a most violent tempest", the hunted Wanderer landed at
Rossinish, near the south-eastern corner of Benbecula, on 27th
April, 1746. Here

> they came to an uninhabited hut where they made a fire to dry their
> cloaths, for all of them were wet through and through in to the
> skin, and an old sail was spread upon the bare ground, which served
> for a bed to the Prince, who was very well pleased with it, and slept
> soundly. Here they kill'd a cow, and the pot which Donald[1] had
> brought served them in good stead for boyling bits of the beef. In
> this poor hut they remained two days and two nights.

On the 29th the fugitives set sail for Stornoway, but were
driven by stress of weather to seek refuge in the islet of Scalpay,
at the entry to East Loch Tarbert. Here, arriving cold, wet and
hungry in the darkness of an early morning, they were hospitably
entertained, in the guise of shipwrecked merchants, by the tacksman of the island, Donald Campbell. The faithful Donald Mac-
Leod was sent forward to Stornoway, in order to hire a vessel to
take the Prince to safer shores. On 3rd May a message was received from him announcing his success in this enterprise. Next
day the Wanderer set out in an open rowing boat: but, once
again, stress of weather drove the little party to seek asylum in
Loch Seaforth, whence, after a long toilsome march of a day and
a night, amid wind and rain, they arrived drenched to the skin,
at Stornoway (5th May). Outside the town they halted in the
sodden moorland, and sent on a messenger to Donald MacLeod,
who forthwith came out with a bottle of brandy and some bread
and cheese. More cheering even than the food and drink was the
news he brought, namely, that Mrs Mackenzie of Arnish would
receive the Wanderer in her house. When the Prince arrived, he

[1] Donald Macleod of Galtrigil, on Loch Dunvegan, the "faithful Palinurus"
of the fugitive Prince.

was obliged to throw off his shirt, which one of the company did wring upon the hearth-stone, and did spread it upon a chair before the fire to have it dried.

Next day brought alarming news. One of the Prince's party, having drunk too much in Stornoway, blabbed that the vessel which Donald MacLeod had chartered was for the service of His Royal Highness. It was said that the Prince had five hundred men with him, and if need be would seize the vessel perforce. Naturally enough, the good folk of Stornoway feared the vengeance of the Government, if their burgh should become the scene of any such escapade. By working alike upon their open fears and secret sympathies, the astute Donald at last prevailed upon the excited burghers to allow the royal fugitive peacefully to quit their town. So the Prince and his party, with a crew of six, set out next morning (6th May) in the same boat which had landed them in Loch Seaforth, and had meantime come round to Stornoway. The appearance of sails thought to be those of Hanoverian warships drove them ashore upon the islet of Iubhard, at the mouth of Loch Shell. The few fishermen there fled inland on their approach, thinking them to be the press gang. Here the fugitives found shelter

in a low pityfull hut, which the fishers had made up for themselves: but it was so ill-roofed that they were obliged to spread the sail of the boat over the top of it. They found heath and turf [peat] enough to make a fire of: but had nothing but the bare ground to lie along when disposed to take a nap, without any covering on them at all.

In this squalid abode the party remained four days and nights, under circumstances hopeless enough yet comforted by the brandy which their kind hostess at Arnish had given them, and by the fish that they found in the hut, or spread out to dry on the shore. When they quitted the island, the Prince wanted to leave money to pay for the fish, but was restrained by his companions for fear that this would arouse suspicions of their real character.

On 10th May the Prince and his faithful few set out for Scalpay, only to find that their host there, Donald Campbell, had "gone a skulking", for the news had got abroad that he had befriended the Wanderer. Coasting along North Uist, in constant danger from English ships, and after spending three wretched nights at Loch Uskevagh in Benbecula, they landed finally (14th May) at Corradale in South Uist. On this island they hid themselves successfully for over a fortnight, and then returned to Benbecula. Here the old Chief of Clanranald, who himself had kept aloof from the Rising, though his son had "been out", brought the miserable Prince clean shirts, shoes and stockings, and welcome supply of Spanish wine.

Meantime the hue and cry, following upon the indiscretions of the drunkard at Stornoway, had become so intense that it was judged advisable for the Prince to go into cover again amid the moorlands of South Uist. Here he remained in comparative safety and comfort for several weeks, amusing himself with fowling and fishing, and entertaining his visitors. In true Ossianic fashion, the Prince drank his brandy out of a scallop shell. Let it be remembered, to the eternal glory of the Gael, that though scores of them (including many non-Jacobites) knew of the Prince's wanderings within their bounds, and although a reward of £30,000—wealth beyond the dreams of avarice in any Highland peasant's imagination—was placed by Government upon his royal head, no person, save one base minister (of whom I have already written) and a wretched starveling boy whom the Prince had befriended, and whose story, fortunately, nobody believed, ever gave a hint of the presence of "the Young Gentleman" in their midst.

At Corradale a spring is still pointed out, whose water the parched Prince found so delicious that he christened it "the Well of the Rock of Wine".

On 6th June the Wanderer quitted Corradale, and after spending four nights at Wiay and two at Rossinish in Benbecula, he was taken back again (13th June) by sea, dodging two English warships to South Uist. In the remarkable ruin of Castle Calvay (of which more hereafter) at the entry to Loch Boisdale, they skulked for fear of English landing parties, comforted, however, by a supply of brandy provided by Lady Boisdale. Around him now, on sea and land, were two English warships and some five hundred soldiers, redcoats and militia. From South Uist the hunted Wanderer crossed once again to Benbecula; and here, at midnight on 21st June, he was introduced to Flora Macdonald, who, though herself no Jacobite, undertook, to her undying glory, the perilous task of conducting him over the sea from Benbecula to Skye. At eight o'clock on 28th June, 1746, "in a very clear evening", the little party consisting of Flora Macdonald, Prince Charles, disguised as her maid, "Betty Burke", her man servant Neil McKechan, and six rowers, set out on their immortal voyage.

How far many of those who thus risked their all in the deadly game of befriending the fugitive Prince were from being uncritical, romantic supporters of the Stuart cause is strikingly brought out by the report of a remarkable conversation which Hugh Macdonald of Balshair in North Uist, had with the Prince at Corradale:—

I starts the question if His Highness would take it amiss if I should tell him the greatest objections against him in Great Britain. He said not. I told him that popery and arbitrary government were the two chiefest. He said it was only bad construction his enemies put on't. "Do you know, Mr Macdonald," he says, "what religion are all the Princes in Europe of?" I told him I imagined they were of the same established religion of the nations they lived in. He told me they had little or no religion at all. Boisdale then told him that his predecessor, Donald Clanranald, had fought seven set battles for his; yet, after the Restoration, he was not owned by King Charles at court. The Prince said, "Boisdale, don't be rubbing up old sores, for if I came home, the case would be otherwise with me." I then says to him that, notwithstanding of what freedom we enjoyed there with him, we could have no access to him if he was settled at London; and he told us then, if he had never so much ado, he'd be one night merry with his Highland friends.

The same narrator has preserved for us this vivid portrait of the Prince as he appeared during his sojourn at Corradale:

His dress was then a tartan short-coat and vest of the same, got from Lady Clanranald, his night cap all patched with soot-drops:[1] his shirt, hands and face all patched with the same: a short kilt, tartan hose, and Highland brogues: his upper coat being English cloth.

South Uist

This long and narrow island, about 22 miles in length and somewhat under 8 miles in greatest width, prolongs the chain of the Outer Hebrides from Benbecula towards Barra, from which it is separated by a sound about 7 or 8 miles broad, wherein are several islets, of which the largest, Eriskay, is of historical importance! The geology and scenery of South Uist answer to the genera. pattern of the Long Island; except that here, after the comparatively flat moorlands of North Uist and Benbecula, we are once more confronted with mountain country, culminating in Hekla

[1] i.e., rain fallings through the leaky, soot-laden thatch of the "black houses".

(1,988 feet) and Ben More (2,034 feet)—whose names, Norse and Celtic respectively, remind us of the double main-stream in the population of the island. Conformably to the usual pattern of the Outer Hebrides, the west coast of South Uist is low, sandy and uninterrupted by sea-lochs, except at the northern end, where Loch Bee, about 2 fathoms in greatest depth, indents the coastline to a length of about 3 miles and an average breadth of perhaps 1 mile. Here good sea-trout fishing may be enjoyed. By contrast, on the eastern littoral the coast is wild, irregular and rocky, though unencumbered with islets. It is breached by three considerable lochs: from north to south, respectively, Loch Skiport, Loch Eynort and Loch Boisdale. Loch Skiport is in practical communication with Loch Bee on the opposite side, and the two between them in effect cut off the northern portion of the island, known as Iachdar. This part of South Uist, with its numerous tarns, inlets and skerries, is really, geomorphically considered, a continuation of Benbecula. In their season, the tarns are gay with water-lilies, and the bare grey rock surfaces are relieved by glowing splashes of golden lichen. A more dismal impression is conveyed by the broad stretches of sullen black bog, nurseries of future peat, amidst which, here and there, green patches tell of byegone shielings. On the southern skirt of Ben More is a small plantation, in season gay with modest woodland flowers.

Loch Eynort is about 6 miles in length, and therefore almost bisects the island. Altogether more important is Loch Boisdale, a notable harbour and the port of South Uist. It is 4 miles long and a good mile in width at the mouth. Within, its wide expanding circuit embraces many islets, the haunt of aquatic birds. At Loch Boisdale the MacBrayne motor vessel *Claymore* calls on Mondays, Wednesdays and Fridays. The little port has a good hotel, a bank and shops, while there are inns at Pollacher, near the south end of the island, and at Carnan, where the bridge from Benbecula introduces the motorist or wayfarer to South Uist. At Eachar, near Carnan, a "black house" has been fitted up as a folk museum. The incongruities of modern life are startlingly thrust upon our attention by the rocket range at Geirinish and the Nature Conservancy's Reserve at Stilligary. On the south-western shore, opposite Isle Orosay, is a seaweed factory, reviving, for different purposes, the old kelp industry.

For the rest, South Uist is a crofting country, famous for its Highland cattle; but it has much to offer the visitor—excellent brown trout and salmon fishing, a good nine-hole golf course at Askernish, safe bathing beaches of glistening white sand on the western coast, a wonderful variety of plant life, and superb opportunities for the bird watcher. In particular, Loch Druidibeg, within the Nature Conservancy, is the chief breeding place in Britain for the graylag goose. Today, South Uist at long last enjoys a reasonably good road system, and is linked by ferries with Eriskay and Barra to the south.

In South Uist, we are in the heart of the Catholic Hebrides. Visible proof of this confronts us in the fine church at Bornish, as also in the great statue of Our Lady of the Isles and the Holy Child, designed by Hew Lorimer, which crowns Rueval Hill, about 4 miles south of Carnan. Inevitably, we find in South Uist that the ancient joyous culture of the Gael has survived, in this kindly spiritual climate, to a greater extent than in the bleak Calvinistic north. South Uist is still renowned for its pipers, and the July festival attracts the most skilful contestants in the Hebrides.

In the north-western corner of the island, on the shore of *Loch-an-duin-mohr* is an area of reeds which no man ever cut, despite the use to which the material could be put for thatching. The reason given for this abstinence is that they are of the same species as that of the reed upon which Stephaton proffered to Our Lord, as He hung dying on the Cross, the sponge dipped in vinegar. So the reeds remain inviolate, for it would be impious to cut them.

In the middle district of South Uist, towards the west, is Howmore, the ancient ecclesiastical centre of the Island. Uncharitably, this was in former days described as "the township of worst manners" in South Uist. It is certainly not that today: and indeed nowhere in South Uist, any less than elsewhere in the Hebrides, will you find anything but the characteristic courtesy, considerateness and frank hospitality of the Highlander.

The ecclesiastical centre of South Uist consisted, in characteristically Celtic fashion, of a group of five churches or chapels. Of these one had long since disappeared, and the others are in sad disarray. The two principal churches were under the invocation respectively of St Mary and St Columba. Of the former church, which measured about 66 feet in overall length and 26 feet 9 inches broad, the east gable retains two interesting windows with external lintels and rear arches slightly pointed in form, but of rough construction; on either side is an aumbry. St Columba's Church

has a single window of much the same character. Of the chapels
not much need here be said: but in one of them is preserved a
remarkable heraldic stone. It shows on the dexter side, a lymphad or sailed galley, above which a hand displays a Celtic cross,
wheeled and shafted, with the arms projecting beyond the wheel
in the Irish manner: on the sinister side a castle or tower with
triple gabled or pyramidal roofs, and above it what looks like
a lion rampant; and in chief a bird perched upon a tree.

There are other ancient church sites in South Uist, but space
forbids us to say anything about them here. The island also contains two ruined castles. One of them, Castle Calvay, is of high
interest. It stands on a rocky islet at the mouth of Loch Boisdale,
and its long swart menacing crenellated wall immediately strikes
the observer as something quite different from the usual tall gaunt
Hebridean or West Highland tower. In fact it is a castle of *enceinte*,
with walls as much as 5 feet thick. At the south-west corner is a
small strong square tower containing a "pit" or dungeon; on the
north side was the *camera* or hall-house with a postern; and midway in the south front, recessed in an embayment of the curtain,
is the portal, secured by a drawbar. Some traces of battlements
remain, and look to be of early type. Moreover, the masonry,
rubble-built with shell-lime mortar, is faced here and there with
slabs set on edge, after an early fashion which we shall have to
consider in more detail at Castle Kisimul (pp. 163–4). In front of
the entrance is a rock-cut wall.

Though its history seems to be a blank, there is no reason known
to me why Castle Calvay should not date back to the thirteenth
or fourteenth century. It was in this bleak and lonely ruin that
Prince Charles Edward lurked for some nights in June 1746, as
described above (page 150).

By contrast, Ormaclett Castle, also now a ruin, is nothing more
than an unfortified laird's house of the early eighteenth century.
It stands between Loch Boisdale and Howmore, but nearer the
latter, and was a residence of Clanranald, built in 1701 and
burned, it would seem accidentally, in 1715—it is said, on the
very day of Sheriffmuir. Above the door is a coat of arms similar
to that on the heraldic stone at Howmore, but with the charges
inverted. The building is made of field gatherings, with freestone
dressings brought from elsewhere; the roofing slabs, some of
which lie about in the ruins, are green mylonite flags from Stuley
Island on the east coast of South Uist.

Stuley Island may give us our first opportunity to talk about a major geological feature in the otherwise somewhat monotonous structure of the Long Island. This is a great fracture, accompanied by movement on a scale to form what is known as a thrust plane, extending from the Butt of Lewis along the entire eastern side of the Long Island as far as the Barra islets. The intensity of the movement, which is believed to have begun in pre-Torridonian times, has produced a whole suite of crush rocks all down the line, of which these mylonites on Stuley Island are an instance. We shall meet with crush rocks of a different kind, in the same zone of fracture, at Castle Kisimul.

At Milton, on the west side of the island, is the birth place of Flora Macdonald. The house where she first saw the light in 1722, her father being tacksman there, is now gone to wreck and ruin, but a cairn with a bronze inscribed plaque commemorates the heroine. It is said that her first meeting with the royal Fugitive was at Alisary, near Ormaclett Castle.

Another famous person connected with South Uist was Jacques Etienne Joseph Alexandre Macdonald, Duke of Taranto, one of Napoleon's marshals, whose father lived at Howmore. The elder Macdonald's Jacobite proclivities had necessitated his withdrawal to France, and the future marshal was born at Sedan. His brilliant career in the Revolutionary and Napoleonic wars is a matter of European history. No less remarkable, amid all the manifold temptations of a scambling and unquiet time, is his loyal and upright character. In 1826 the Marshal paid a visit to his father's house. From the ancestral soil he took back a boxful of earth, and in his grave at Courcelles-le-Roi it was buried with him.

The prehistoric antiquities of South Uist—cairns, wheel-houses, duns and brochs—do not differ in any wise from those common to the Long Island.

Eriskay

Between South Uist and Barra lies the little island of Eriskay. In itself it is in no way distinguished. It is but a storm-beaten chunk of gneiss, about 3 miles long and half that in breadth. Nevertheless, the islet has an imperishable place in Scottish history: for here, on 23rd July, 1745, landed Prince Charles Edward Stuart, to project himself forth, with no more than a single shipload of companions, upon what was perhaps the most heroic and foolhardy venture in the whole long course of British history:

When they landed in Eriska, they could not find a grain of meal or one inch of bread. But they catched some flounders, which they roasted upon the bare coals in a mean, low hut they had gone into near the shore, and Duncan Cameron stood cook. The Prince sat at the cheek of the little ingle, upon a fail sunk [i.e., a bank of peats] and laughed heartily at Duncan's cookery, for he himself owned he played his part awkwardly enough.

The very first night they landed happened to prove violently stormy and wet, and they were obliged to lodge in one of the little country houses, wherein there were already many others that were weather bound.

Here they were all refreshed as well as the place could afford, and they had some beds, but not sufficient for the whole company, on which account the Prince, being less fatigued than the others, insisted upon such to go to bed as most wanted it. Particularly he took care of Sir Thomas Sheridan, and went to examine his bed, to see that the sheets were well aired. The landlord, observing him to search the bed so narrowly, and at the same time hearing him declare he would sit up all night, called out to him, and said it was so good a bed, and the sheets were so good, that a prince need not be ashamed to lie in them.

The Prince, not being accustomed to such fires in the middle of the room, and there being no other chimney than a hole in the roof, was almost choaked, and was obliged to go often to the door for fresh air. This at last made the landlord, Angus MacDonald,[1] call out, "What a plague is the matter with that fellow, that he can neither sit nor stand still, and neither keep within nor without doors."

Prince Charles's Beach, where the Young Adventurer landed in such unpropitious circumstances, is a marvellous stretch of shell sand, in bright sunshine of an almost pearly hue, on the western side of the island. Behind it the *machair* is gay with convolvulus, which tradition associated with the Prince's landing. The "black house" in which he spent his first night on the soil of his ancestral kingdom survived until 1902, when it was unfeelingly demolished. Here is a description of it in the last year of its survival:

It is just like a score more within a stone's throw, and has probably changed little in a century and a half. An iron pot is boiling over a peat fire in the middle of the clay floor, the roof is black with smoke, the family beds are in cupboards concealed by dimity cur-

[1] The tacksman of Eriskay.

tains; hens are clucking to call attention to the eggs thay have deposited in corners: wooden trunks are ranged along the wall containing all possessions that are not in actual use, and a bench made of a plank supported on rocks is the most noticeable article of furniture. A small dresser, adorned with gay crockery, speaks of relations with the mainland, visits probably to the east-coast fishing, and is the only article which could not have been present when Prince Charlie stood here, coughing at the peat smoke, as we do today.[1]

The chain from which the pot is suspended from the roof over the central fire has been the subject of strange superstition in Eriskay. It is said to be the special property of the Devil, who is referred to as "Him of the Chain". Therefore the chain should be handled as little as possible. The magical properties of iron, as a protection against spells and malign influences, are of course the subject of superstitions widely prevalent throughout the world: but it seems unusual to find the metal regarded as of ominous import.

The population of Eriskay number about 300, and are mainly engaged in herring, lobster, and prawn fishing. Practically all of them belong to the ancient faith. Administratively, the island is attached to South Uist.

South of Eriskay lies Weaver's Island, a lump of rock shaped somewhat like an hour glass. The southern lobe forms a lofty stack, and is crowned by the stump of a small oblong tower, strongly built of random rubble and shell-lime. From the tower a splendid view is obtained over Barra, Eriskay and South Uist. Moreover, the place is an unrivalled stance for "spotting" migrant sea-birds.

This is the "Weaver's Castle", concerning which some weird legends are current. "The Weaver" is said to have been a Macneil who made things so hot for himself by wrecking and piracy that he built this inaccessible tower as a hideout. When it was finished, he crossed over to South Uist and there stole a girl out of a shieling, whom he carried back to his eyrie to become his wife. The lass is said to have been a weaver, and so the tower got its name. Anyhow, she soon became an accomplice of her husband in his lawless enterprises. When boats sheltered in the Sound of Eriskay or in Barra Sound, so it is said, the pair cut the hawsers and let the vessel drift to wreck upon the rocky shores, whereupon they

[1] A. Goodrich-Freer, *Outer Isles*, pp. 263-4.

helped themselves to its contents. At last their depredations became so intolerable that an expedition was despatched against the wreckers. "The Weaver" and his three sons were surprised on Eriskay and all put to death. But a fourth son, "the little Weaver", survived; and the story of his subsequent adventurous career, and how in due course he tracked down and murdered his father's slayer, is one of the best of the "Tales told by the Coddy", whereof more hereafter (see p. 171).

In modern times, Eriskay Sound has become famous through the wreck, in February, 1941, on Hartamul rock at its eastern inlet, of the 12,000 ton cargo ship *Politician*, on its way to America with a consignment of whisky—24,000 cases, or 243,000 bottles! The story of how the Hebrideans, hastening to the scene from near and far, relieved the stranded vessel of her contents, and of the effect which this glorious windfall exerted upon the plunderers, has been immortalized by Sir Compton Mackenzie in his hilarious (yet how subtle!) novel, *Whisky Galore*, and in the film based thereon, which between them have made the Saga of the "Polly" familiar to uncounted thousands all over the English speaking world.

IX

BARRA

The most southerly of the larger islands that together form the
Long Island group is Barra. In the opinion of not a few lovers of
the Outer Hebrides, it is the most charming of them all. Irregular
in outline, with its rocky and rifted coast indented by several
large sandy bays, the island is of considerable size, measuring some
eight miles in length by five miles in greatest breadth. The rocks
are composed of Lewisian gneiss, rising into bold, craggy, or peat-
covered hills, of which the highest is Heaval (1,260 feet). Generally
speaking, however, the surface is grassy, and there is not much
heather. Barra includes some rich pasture-land and meadows,
cultivated by a hardy crofting population; while at Castlebay,
the only sizeable township, there is still a certain amount of fishing.
As elsewhere, the crofters are now comfortably housed in neat
white cottages, and an ample supply of water has been provided
by a dam thrown across Loch an Duin, in the northern portion
of the island, and also from Loch Uisge just above Castlebay.
Barra, however, still awaits its electricity, though there are a
number of private generating plants. The installation of the
electrical system was begun in September, 1965. A few of the old
"black houses" continue to be occupied, and are kept with
scrupulous neatness. In these, reeds or corn stalks are now used
for thatch, in place of bent, the ancient material. There is little
peat, and imported coal is the principal fuel. The population of
the island numbers about 1,400.

The glory of Barra consists in its beaches. Nowhere else in the
Hebrides are the sands of more dazzling whiteness. When the tide
is in, the range of colour on a fine day becomes of great and varied
beauty—a lovely green or sometimes a pale gold over the sand,
purple above the beds of seaweed, rich brown where peaty
streams pay their tribute to the sea. By far the most spectacular
beach is the *Traigh Mhor* (Great Strand), near the northern end of

the island, on its eastern side. Here a wide and deep embayment reduces the island to a narrow neck, bounded on the Atlantic side by a range of bold sand dunes, brilliantly white, but crested with crisp turf or coarse bent. Beyond this the northern apex of Barra again becomes rocky and rugged, rising into two summits dignified by the names of Ben Eoligarry and Ben Scurrival—though the term "ben" may seem somewhat pretentious, since the higher, Ben Eoligarry, is no more than 338 feet in height. The Department of Agriculture, which owns this portion of the island, has developed a crofting township at Eoligarry and is embarking on a policy of plantation.

On the "Cockle Ebb" in *Traigh Mhor* is the Barra airfield, which surely must be one of the most remarkable in Britain. Once a day from April to September, and thrice weekly (weather permitting) during the winter, the tiny aircraft lands and leaves, its timetable being regulated by the tides. Over the hard, firm, ripple-marked sand, sometimes splashing through shallow water, the plane taxies towards the airport offices, if the term may be applied to a single building no larger than a Boy Scout troop headquarters. The staff here consists of a lady, probably the only woman superintendent of an airport in Europe, and a man of all work. A fire engine stands by when the plane is grounded—or, one should rather say, beached.

On *Traigh Mhor* delicious cockles are collected. Their fame is of long standing. A traveller of 1549 claims that "ther is na fairer and more profitable sands for cokills in all the world." Gravely he informs his readers that these cockles are engendered, no bigger than a grain of corn, in a fresh water spring on top of a hill overlooking the Bay, whence they descend by a burn and grown to their full size in the Cockle Ebb! In 1794 it is recorded that

> during the last two summers, which were particularly distressing on account of the great scarcity, no less than 100 to 200 horse-loads of cockles were taken off the sands at low water every day of the spring tides during the months of May, June, July and August.

At Vaslain, behind *Traigh Mhor*, is a small but interesting industry, the manufacture of shell-grit, used for harling. The shells have a high lime content and are extremely white, so the rough-cast which they produce is at once durable and comely. The shell-grit is also fed to chickens.

A single-track ring road, 14 miles in length, has been construc-

In the seaweed factory, South Uist

ted round the central portion of the island, the work being completed in 1939.

The centre of life in Barra is Castlebay. This most attractive township is sprawled out, with true Hebridean *insouciance*, on the bluff grassy slopes leading down to a capacious basin, in which large vessels can find shelter in stormy weather. The little village is dominated by the handsome Roman Catholic Church, completed in 1889, and under the charming invocation of Our Lady, Star of the Sea. With its imposing tower, arcaded nave and aisles, the church has almost a cathedral-like aspect in the prevailing small scale of island scenery and buildings. The texts on the two altar frontals, and the descriptions on the Stations of the Cross, are all in Gaelic, which, it need hardly be said, is almost universally spoken on the island. Most of the population belong to the ancient faith, to which they have staunchly clung alike amidst neglect and persecution. The Church of Rome now maintains five places of worship in Barra. The Church of Scotland has two. The village boasts a couple of hotels, and is well provided with the usual amenities, including a tennis court. Sea fishing and boating excursions are available, and the few fresh water lochs on the island have recently been re-stocked with trout under the auspices of the Scottish Tourist Board. The Barra folk impress the stranger in their midst as an intensely live community, full of schemes for the advancement of their lovely island.

From whatever standpoint you look out over Castlebay the lovely, almost land-locked basin is dominated by the imposing pile of Kisimul Castle, perched on its rock in the middle of the bay. So completely does it occupy its area that at high tide the waves lap the base of the castle walls. In itself, the rock is of much geological interest. It is formed out of a mass of black flinty crush-rock, which by reason of its extreme hardness and durability has successfully resisted the increasing battery of "the wild and wasteful waves of ocean"—until in the fulness of time it was selected as the *assiette* of the most significant and interesting castle in all the Hebrides. By "flinty crush-rock" is denoted a dark, almost vitreous material, formed by the intense and prolonged crushing, under enormous stresses far beneath the earth's surface, of a metamorphic rock such as schist or gneiss. Usually it occurs where movement has taken place along a line of faulting or fracture in the earth's crust. Here at Barra it is no doubt the product of a great fault, or thrust-plane, which runs down the

11

Silverweed, Potentilla anserina, *Uist*

whole eastern side of the Long Island group (see p. 155). The magnitude of movement and pressure made the gneiss, hard and durable as it was in its original state, viscous and indeed almost molten, so that it recrystallized in a glass-like mass. Owing to its dense covering with slippery tangle, the castle rock, even when the tide is low, cannot be closely studied; but fortunately a good exposure of the same material is available close east of Castlebay pier.

Kisimul Castle owes its presence and its importance to the fine natural harbour of Castlebay. In the days when Norway owned the Orkneys and the Shetlands, the Hebrides and the Isle of Man, and a large domain in Ireland, Barra with its safe and capacious anchorage became a half-way staging post on the outer maritime route from the mother country to its far flung western dependencies—from Bergen to Dublin, Wexford, Waterford and Limerick. It is significant that, of the four Norse graves recorded from the Outer Hebrides, two were found in Barra and one in adjoining Eriskay. From the Eriskay burial came the fragments of a Viking sword; those in Barra yielded remains of swords and shields, also brooches and buckles, combs and a whetstone—all well-known items in the kit of a viking warrior.

Reference has already been made (*supra*, p. 17) to the frequent mention of Barra in the Sagas. Even more interesting is the preservation, in the Icelandic *Edda*, a collection of early Norse literature, of some fragments of verse of a Norse-Hebridean poet, Orm of Barra.

From time immemorial "Kisimul's Castle, our ancient glory" has been the seat of the Macneils of Barra. Since 1938 the late Chief, by profession an architect and by instinct and training a scholar and antiquary, was engaged with unfaltering patience and persistence, in spite of the Second World War and all the manifold difficulties and distractions of our times, in restoring the stronghold of his forebears and making it once more into a habitable dwelling. His achievement is the more remarkable because he was born and bred an American, and came over to Barra only for the building season. He always retained the British citizenship derived through his father. What he accomplished is both scholarly and restrained, and in its earlier phases was carried out under the advice and with the assistance of the Ancient Monuments Division of the Ministry of Public Building and Works. In no essential particular have the ancient and distinctive features of the building been destroyed or needlessly obscured; and a full photographic record is available of the state of the ruins before the work began.

Like the other early medieval strongholds of the Western Seaboard and the Hebrides, Kisimul Castle began as a great curtain or ring wall, adjusted to the contours of the seagirt rock. Midway in the eastern front was the only entrance, defended by a portcullis. Later, a great *donjon*, or square keep tower, lofty and browbeating, and rising from a boldly spreading plinth, was inserted on the south-eastern side. The original entrance was then blocked up, and a new portal, defended not by a portcullis but by a machicolated jutty overhead, was made close up to the keep, so as to be under its immediate surveillance. Within the courtyard are a hall, chapel and other buildings, now restored by The Macneil.

Both the curtain wall and the great tower retain, in a degree of perfection unique in Scotland, and indeed with few equals in Britain, the early medieval arrangements for crowning the wall-heads with wooden galleries, designed for defence. Such timber war-heads were known as *bretasches* or *hourds*. Except where provision had to be made for manning the portcullis at the original gate, there was no parapet walk on the curtain. Instead, the inner face of the wall exhibits a scarcement, while the walls are pierced with a series of putlog holes. The scarcement and putlog holes supported a wooden gallery with a penthouse roof. This gallery projected on both sides of the wall. Along the inside gallery the defenders moved freely and in safety round the castle. To the outer gallery they had access through a series of deep embrasures in the wall: and from this outer gallery, by means of loopholes in its front and *meurtrières* or "murder-holes" in its floor, they could discharge or hurl down missiles or offensive materials upon the assailants struggling precariously to establish themselves on the slippery rocks below. Such timber war-heads are characteristic of twelfth and thirteenth century military construction in western Europe, before the time when stone corbels carrying oversailing machicolated parapets came into general use. Though the thick walls of the great tower are crowned with a regular *allure* or wall-walk, this also was provided with a timber war-head similar to those on the curtain.

A conspicuous feature of the masonry at Kisimul Castle, both in the curtain and in the tower, is the tendency to build with bands of large stones up-ended or set on edge, so as to present their

broad flat surfaces to the exterior. This is a form of building common in early medieval structures in the Hebrides. Probably the
idea was to reduce the penetration of rain—and of course at Kisimul, sea water as well—driven against the walls by high winds
in a wet and stormy climate. The practice may be regarded as
a kind of "cladding" of the wall-face with vertical slates or flag-
stones. Doubtless it originated in church buildings, where the
walls are thinner than those of the castles, and damp penetrating
through them might spoil painted plaster inside.

Upon all counts it is clear that while Kisimul Castle is the work
of Hebridean masons, the master mason or deviser of the building—the architect as we should nowadays call him—was well
abreast of current military practice. In this there is no cause for
surprise: for, as I have shown elsewhere, the greater island chiefs
were in full contact with the wide world beyond, and well able,
in their building enterprises, to import a *maistre maçon de franch
peer* from one of the great centres of Romanesque or Gothic
design.[1]

The Macneils of Barra took themselves very seriously. It is
recorded that after the Chief had finished his midday meal, a
herald mounted the great tower of Kisimul Castle, and, after a
flourish on his trumpet, proclaimed to all the world: "Hear, ye
people, and listen, ye nations! The Macneil of Barra having
finished his dinner, all the princes of the earth are at liberty to
dine!" It is further recorded that the Chief of the day refused
Noah's offer of hospitality because the Macneil of Barra had a boat
of his own! An amusing account of his reception at Kisimul is
given by the traveller Martin Martin, who visited Barra in 1695:

There is a stone wall round it two storeys high, reaching the sea,
and within the wall there is an old tower and a hall, with other
houses about it. There is a little magazine in the tower, to
which no stranger has access. I saw the officer called the Cockman[2]
and an old cock he is; when I bid him ferry me over the water
to the island, he told me he was but an inferior officer, his
business being to attend in the tower; but if (says he) the constable, who then stood on the wall, will give you access, I'll ferry
you over. I desired him to procure me the constable's permission,

---

[1] See on this subject my book *The Castle of Bergen and the Bishop's Palace at
Kirkwall*. (1961).
[2] Gokman, i.e. "look-out man".

and I would reward him; but having waited some hours for the constable's answer, and not receiving any, I was obliged to return without seeing this famous fort. Macneil and his lady being absent was the cause of this difficulty, and of my not seeing the place. I was told some weeks after that the constable was very apprehensive of some design I might have in viewing the fort, and thereby to expose it to the conquest of a foreign power, of which I supposed there was no great cause of fear.

Before unduly ridiculing the officiousness of the Constable of Kisimul, let us remember that in the year of Martin's visit the Revolution of 1689, which hurled the Stewarts from their throne, was no more than seven years old; that the Macneils of Barra were staunch supporters of the fallen dynasty; that the Scottish Jacobites were deeply involved in secret dealings with France; that the air in the Highlands and Islands was thick with rumours of plot and counterplot: and that the Constable may well have suspected that the stranger's unheralded visit could be a prelude to a proposal to place a Williamite garrison in Kisimul—which the faithful Constable unquestionably would have regarded as "the conquest of the Castle by a foreign power".

A grand story is told about "Roderick the Turbulent", the Chief of Clan Neil during the reign of James VI. He had seized an English vessel off the shores of Ireland. Queen Elizabeth complained to the Scottish monarch about this act of piracy. The Macneil was summoned to appear befory the Privy Council in Edinburgh to answer for his conduct. But the island potentate ignored the royal command, so a vessel was sent to fetch him. This problem, however, was easier posed than solved. A solution was found by the simple expedient of inviting the Chief on board, making him drunk, and carrying him off. Confronted in Edinburgh with the question, why had he committed an unprovoked assault on the vessel of a friendly sovereign, Macneil replied that he imagined he had done the King a service by injuring "the woman who had murdered His Majesty's mother". So taken aback was King James by this forthright rejoinder that, instead of ordering the turbulent chief to the gallows, he contented himself with forfeiting his island estate. It was, however, soon restored to him by the grantee, Mackenzie of Kintail, who nevertheless retained the superiority, Macneil being bound to pay an annual rent of £20 Scotch money—in sterling £3 6s. 8d.—plus a hawk when required. Later, the superiority passed to the Macdonalds of Sleat, now represented by Lord Macdonald of Armadale, with whom it still nominally remains.

In 1795 Kisimul Castle was accidentally burned. In 1838 the then Macneil, or rather his trustees in bankruptcy, sold Barra to Colonel Gordon of Cluny: but in 1937 the greater portion, extending to some 12,000 acres, was bought back by the present Chief.[1] As already stated, the northern tip belongs to the Ministry of Agriculture and Fisheries.

In this northern tip are the ruined parish church and burial place of Kilbar (*Cillebharra*) St Barr's Church. In Celtic and medieval times this was the most important ecclesiastical centre on the island, a sanctuary and place of pilgrimage much visited from near and far. The cemetery with its church and two small attendant chapels—a grouping highly characteristic of Celtic practice—is most beautifully situated on the eastern skirt of Ben Eoligarry. It commands a wide and varied prospect over the Sound of Fuday and the Sound of Barra, the adjacent green islets of Fuday and Eriskay—noted winter haunts of the barnacle goose—and in the background the South Uist hills, bare, brown and lumpish. All three buildings seem more or less of the same date, and that an early one. The door of the parish church has inclined jambs in the Irish manner, and the windows (mere slits) have round arches cut in a single stone. Another Irish mannerism is the triangular heads, formed of two stones tilted against each other, found on the main door and over the inner side of the splayed windows. Formerly there was a third attendant chapel, long since removed.

Lying in the churchyard, unkempt as always in the Hebrides, three fine sculptured monuments of the usual West Highland type remain, uncared for amid the rank tangled grass. A fourth is on record, but is probably sunk beneath the all-devouring turf. Two of the visible gravestones display the usual claymore, set against a rich and intricate background of leafy scroll-work, passing upward, in one case into an interlaced pattern of typical Celtic design, and in the other into a beautiful eight-armed cross of foliage. The third slab shows no sword, but a lymphad or masted galley, set amid a complicated pattern of leaf scrolls, while below is the ancient Celtic motive of the deer pursued by a hound. These

[1] For those interested in more detail about the history and restoration of Kisimul Castle, reference may be made to The Macneil's book, *Castle in the Sea*, which is a distinctive and important contribution to the neglected history of the Hebrides.

three slabs are of quite unearthly beauty. At present they lie exposed to the weather, the assaults of birds, and the boots of thoughtless visitors. They should be removed to the now restored chapel of Kisimul Castle, and fixed upright against the side walls of its chancel.

Another stone from this famous Celtic sanctuary is now safely housed in the National Museum of Antiquities. It is of unique importance as the only runic inscribed stone thus far recorded from the Hebrides. On the front it bears a somewhat crude Celtic cross ornamented with degenerate plaitwork, and flanked with escaping spirals and fretwork patterns. On the back is the inscription in runes. The latest rendering of this, by the Norwegian scholar Magnus Olsen, runs thus: "After [i.e. in memory of] Thorgerth Steiner's daughter this cross was erected." This stone dates probably from the eleventh century.

St Barr of Cork, the patron saint of Barra, to whom the island is said to owe its name, is still venerated among the inhabitants. Martin tells us how upon the altar of Kilbar—of which the underbuilding still remains—there stood his wooden image, clad in a linen shirt. Formerly it was the custom on the Saint's day (25th September) for the Barra folk to assemble at Kilbar and ride in solemn procession three times sunwise round the churchyard. Their steeds were ponies, and wives or girl friends were mounted behind the riders.

An ancient Celtic martyrology records this beautiful rhyme about St Barr:

> Barr, the fire of wisdom, loves
> Humility to the men of the world;
> He never saw in want
> A person that he did not assist.

The very ancient and sacred graveyard of Kilbar is still in use, and indeed has recently been extended. No one but the most blatant materialist will under-estimate the comfort of knowing one is to sleep in such hallowed ground. The first glance at the inscriptions will show that the great majority of those commemorated are Catholics. The white painted stones make an immediate and strong impression as you approach the cemetery.

The remaining antiquities of Barra are of minor interest. They include the stump of a small but massive square tower on an islet in Loch Tangusdale; a number of *duns*, one or two of which seem to be degenerate versions of the broch theme; some chambered cairns; and a few standing stones.

Some little time after the burning of Kisimul Castle in 1795, the Macneils of Barra built themselves a house at Eoligarry, which still stands, though untenanted and fast falling into disrepair. This is a pity, as the mansion, three storeys in height, with a high-pitched slated roof, is a dignified example of the domestic architecture of the early nineteenth century. The large walled garden adjoining is likewise in utter neglect. In spring, the braes behind Eoligarry are a veritable carpet of primroses, marvellous to behold.

The paternal despotism exercised by the old-time Chiefs of Barra over their clansmen is strikingly revealed by the following passage from Martin:

> When a tenant's wife in this or the adjacent islands dies, he then addresses himself to Macneil of Barray, representing his loss, and at the same time desires that he would be pleased to recommend a wife to him, without which he cannot manage his affairs, nor beget followers to Macneil, which would prove a public loss to him. Upon this representation, Macneil finds out a suitable match for him; and the woman's name being told him, immediately he goes to her, carrying with him a bottle of strong waters for their entertainment at marriage, which is then consummated.
>
> When a tenant dies, the widow addresseth herself to Macneil in the same manner, who likewise provides her with a husband, and they are married without any further courtship . . .
>
> If a tenant chance to lose his milk cows by the severity of the season, or any other misfortune; in this case Macneil of Barray supplies him with the like number that he lost.
>
> When any of these tenants are so far advanced in years that they are incapable to till the ground, Macneil takes such old men into his own family,[1] and maintains them all their life after.

Such patriarchal government of course was dealt its death-blow by the abolition in 1747 of the heritable jurisdictions. Yet all was not thereby gain, as the penetrating intellect of Samuel Johnson fully understood. The Chiefs, he observes

---

[1] Of course the word family is here used in the more ancient and wider sense, signifying household, which is the meaning of the Latin *familia*. Cf. Wyntoun's Chronicle, bk. IX, 27, 116:—

> "His leve than at the King tuk he
> And com til Brugis in that quhile
> In honoure gret wyth his famyle."

being now deprived of their jurisdiction, have already lost much of
their influence; and as they gradually degenerate from patriarchal
rulers to rapacious landlords, they will divest themselves of the
little that remains.

And again:

The Chiefs, divested of their prerogatives, necessarily turned
their thoughts to the improvement of their revenues, and expect
more rent, as they have less homage. The tenant, who is far from
perceiving that his condition is made better in the same proportion
as that of his landlord is made worse, does not immediately see why
his industry is to be taxed more heavily than before. He refuses to
pay the demand, and is ejected; the ground is then let to a stranger,
who perhaps brings a larger stock, but who, taking the land at its
full price, treats with the Laird upon equal terms, and considers him
not as a Chief, but as a trafficker in land. Thus the estate perhaps
is improved, but the clan is broken.

As elsewhere in the Hebrides, the whole history of Barra since
the "Forty-five", at least up to the beginning of the present century,
goes to prove the large element of truth in these sage observations
of Dr Johnson. In Barra, the decline seems to have begun with
the closing down of the kelp industry in 1822, and with the succession to the Chieftainship, in that same year, of General
Roderick Macneil. The prosperity of the tenants due to kelp had
led, naturally enough, to the raising of their rents. When the
industry failed, the rents were not reduced, with the inevitable
result of widespread distress among the islanders. The Chief himself of course was not exempt from the economic breakdown. In
1827 he became bankrupt, and retired to London. In 1838 his
trustees sold the estate (as already mentioned) to an Aberdeenshire
laird, Gordon of Cluny. Now commenced a long period of absentee landlordism, during which the proprietors dealt with the island
purely as a source of revenue, while doing as little as possible
to alleviate the condition of the rent payers. Emigration, mostly
across the Atlantic, inevitably increased. There followed the tragic
story of the Clearances—in the course of which the proprietor,
Colonel Gordon, offered to sell the island to H.M. Government
for use as a penal colony! Much of the best land was thrown into
large farms, and the crofters who had not emigrated were huddled
together on the poorer patches. An unforeseen further calamity
was the potato famine of 1846. Better times were heralded by the

Crofters' Commission appointed in 1883. Amid all the conflict of evidence and the passion aroused by the inquiry held in Barra, as elsewhere, the reality of the Crofters' grievances stares bleakly forth from the printed pages of the Commission's Reports. Since then, large farms have, slowly but surely, been broken up into small holdings, though illegal squatting on land continued until after the First World War. But nobody today can doubt that the position of the crofters, all over the Hebrides, has immeasurably improved. Unfortunately, in Barra at least, the fishing industry, of which Castlebay was once a bustling centre, is now relatively insignificant.

The best *coup d'oeil* of Barra is obtained by the visitor who scrambles up its highest peak, Heaval. On his ascent from Castlebay he will pass a touching memorial of the Catholic piety of the islanders. This is a statue, in Carrara marble, of the Blessed Virgin and Child, placed here during the Marian Year, 1954. Whether this stone will long endure the climate of Barra is anyone's guess.

The devotion of the Barra folk to the Mother of our Saviour is beautifully expressed in a Gaelic rhyme sung by the fishermen before embarking on the cruel seas. It has been translated thus:

> Father, Son, and Spirit's Might!
> Be the Three-in-one with us, day and night;
> On the crested wave, when waves run high,
> Oh Mother Mary, be to us nigh—
> Oh Mother Mary, be to us nigh!

From Heaval a comprehensive view may be enjoyed of the long chain of green islands which stretches southward a dozen miles from Barra, terminating in Berneray, upon which is the Barra Head lighthouse, built in 1833, and crowning a mighty precipice over 600 feet in height. Close beside the lighthouse is a fine specimen of a galleried *dun*. In medieval times this southern group of islands, though always actually possessed by the Macneils, belonged nominally to the Bishop of Sodor and Man, and are still known as "the Bishop's Isles". They present one of the most superb deployments of rock scenery in all Britain, though only to be explored by boat in calm weather. These stupendous beetling cliffs and yawning chasms, battered and fretted into the most fantastic outlines by the ceaseless onslaught of the wild Atlantic rollers, are the haunt of myriads of seabirds—razor-bills, guillemots, rock-pigeons, sea-gulls, and above all, puffins.

On one of the Bishop's Isles, Pabbay, now uninhabited save by sheep and cattle, but once noted for its rich crop bearing soil, is another of the very few Pictish symbol stones known in the Hebrides (see p. 65). It displays an equal armed cross, below which is the crescent and V-rod symbol, and below this again the so-called "lily" symbol. The sculpture is in outline, and incised.

The red lichen which in the autumn splashes the dark grey rocks of Barra was once believed by the inhabitants to be the blood of fairy hosts battling in the middle air. This weird legend is referred to by Thomson in *The Castle of Indolence*:

> As when a shepherd of the Hebrid Isles,
> Placed far amid the melancholy main,
> (Whether it be lone fancy him beguiles
> Or that aerial beings sometimes deign
> To stand, embodied, to our senses plain),
> Sees on the naked hill, or valley low,
> The whilst in ocean Phoebus dips his wain,
> A vast assembly moving to and fro:
> Then all at once in air dissolves the wonderous show.

Thanks largely to the fact that these two islands have escaped the blight of Calvinism, which has done so much to destroy the ancient graces of life in the Hebrides, Barra and Eriskay, and to a lesser degree South Uist, are probably, in these latter years of our materialistic twentieth century, the last refuge of the immemorial traditions, folk-lore and music of the Isles. Who has not heard of Marjorie Kennedy Fraser and the *Songs of the Hebrides*? Who has not rejoiced to hear her setting of the Eriskay Love-lilt? It has been sung, heard and loved across the five continents and the seven seas. And who, in more recent times, has not been fascinated by the *Tales from Barra*—those marvellous yarns about sea monsters and mermaids, kelpies, ghosts and fairies, brownies, elves, and witches, second sight and divination, ancient wars and ancient loves—all retailed, in his own inimitable salty fashion, either in his native Gaelic or in his quaint idiom of English, by that marvellous character, John Macpherson, familiarly known throughout the Western Isles as "the Coddy"? In recording these, and giving them forth to the world, both in their Gaelic and English garbs, Mr John Lorne Campbell has indeed done a national service by preserving an important and charming element of Scotland's Celtic heritage. "The Coddy" died in his native island in 1955, and rests there in Kilbar Churchyard. As the *Oban Times* wrote of him, in his ancestral tongue, "Give him everlasting rest, O Lord, and light that never fails." His sterling character, richly flavoured personality, versatile talents, and real if home-grown learning, had earned for him a host of friends from near and far, and in many walks of life.

X

ST KILDA

"Placed far amid the melancholy main," some fifty-five miles
west of North Uist, the St Kildan group of islands are the remotest
of the Hebrides, and indeed the remotest part of Great Britain,
with the single exception of Rockall, which lies about a hundred
miles further out—well beyond the "Atlantic shelf". The quotation which begins this section is from James Thomson's *The
Castle of Indolence* (see *supra.* p. 171). His friend David Mallet likewise wrote verse about "remotest Kilda", which he describes as

> Last of the sea-girt Hebrides that guard,
> In filial train, Britannia's parent coast.

Nobody knows the origin of the name St Kilda. No such saint is
on record in the Calendar. The ancient name of the principal
island of the group, which form part of the civil parish of Harris,
and therefore of Inverness-shire, is Hirta; and of this word likewise no certain explanation is forthcoming.

The group consists of four islands. The principal, Hirta,
measures about 2½ miles, east and west, by 1¾ miles transversely,
and comprises some 1,575 acres. Close to the north-west is Soay,
of about 244 acres. To the south-east of Hirta, separated from it
only by a narrow strait, lies Dun, 79 acres. Four miles to the north-
east of Hirta is Boreray, 189 acres. There are also five giant isolated
pinnacles of rock, besides other and smaller stacks, making a total
of some sixteen, apart from smaller stacks and skerries. The whole
group form the dissected fragments of another of those great
Eocene volcanoes of the "Thulean Province", which we have
already discussed *apropos* of Skye and the Small Isles. It is believed
that the basal wreck of this giant volcano, most of which has
foundered beneath the assaults of the Atlantic, must cover an
area of no less than six miles. As in Skye, the centre of igneous
activity moved from west to east, and in the later phase gabbro

was succeeded by granophyre. Thus the scenery varies from the dark rugged splintered western profile of the Cambir on Hirta itself, and in Soay and Boreray, to the smoothly rounded, domical, scree-strewn, buff-coloured outlines of Conachair and Oiseval, reminding us of the Red Hills in Skye. The highest point is Conachair, 1,396 feet. On the north, this hill descends sheer into the Atlantic waves in the highest cliff in all Britain, 1,300 feet of awesome precipice. The cliff scenery of the whole group, whether of gabbro or of granophyre, can be described only as stupendous. Stac an Armin, off Boreray, is the tallest stack in Britain, reaching a height of 627 feet. Equally fantastic are the caves, some of which are as much as a hundred yards in depth. Only on the south side of Hirta, in Village Bay, is there a considerable area of low and fairly level ground, consisting of a storm beach about a quarter of a mile in length. Here, therefore, as the name implies, was the principal settlement. There appears to be little heather, the hills being clothed in peat and mountain grass. Two rivulets, one flowing north and the other south, usually dry up in the rare seasons of drought. They are "mis-fits", and perhaps occupy former glacial valleys.

So far, H.M. Geological Survey have published no full-scale account of the group: and the most convenient sketches, for the general reader, will be found in Sir Archibald Geikie's classical work on *The Ancient Volcanoes of Great Britain*, (1897); in the brief section contributed by the late Dr A. M. Cockburn to John Mathieson's well-known paper on St Kilda in *The Scottish Geographical Magazine* vol. XLIV (1928); and in his own more extensive survey published in the *Transactions of the Royal Society of Edinburgh*, vol. 58 (1935): and in the Geological Survey's Memoir on *The Tertiary Volcanic Districts of Scotland*. Unfortunately the admirable little handbook by Tom Steel, *The Life and Death of St Kilda*, published by the National Trust in 1965, is unaccountably silent about the natural history of the islands. As is well known, the inhabitants were evacuated in 1930, and the St Kilda group are now maintained by the National Trust as a Nature Conservancy. The only permanent inhabitants are now the personnel of an observing station for the Benbecula rocket range. The tale of the Nature Conservancy's splendid pioneer work in safeguarding the wild life of the island has been brilliantly told by Mr Kenneth Williamson and Dr J. Martin Boyd in their fascinating book, *St Kilda Summer* (1960).

At this point it will be proper to make it clear that, beyond seeing it upon the western horizon on a clear day from Harris, I have no personal acquaintance with St Kilda. What I have to say in this section is therefore wholly a compilation: but it has been read by my colleague the late Professor A. C. O'Dell, of the Chair of Geography in the University of Aberdeen, who was well acquainted with the island group.[1]

About the tremendous cliff Conachair Geikie has written with his accustomed eloquence:

> Nowhere among the Inner Hebrides, not even on the south-western side of Rum, is there any such display of the capacity of the youngest granite to assume the most rugged and picturesque forms. It is hardly possible to exaggerate the variety of outline assumed by the rock as it yields along its system of joints to the influence of a tempestuous climate. It has been carved into huge projecting buttresses and deep alcoves, the naked stone glowing with tints of orange and fawn colour, veiled here and there with patches of bright green slope, or edged with fringes of sea-pink and camomile. Every outstanding bastion is rent with chasms and split into blocks, which accumulate on the ledges like piles of ruined walls. To one who boats underneath these cliffs the scene of ceaseless destruction which they present is vividly impressive.

In the second phase of Phlegrean action, when the granophyre thrust itself up into the overlying gabbro masses, it was in an extremely liquid state. As a result, it injected itself into the older rock in innumerable dykes, sheets, veins and even threads and "stringers", so multiplied and intricate as sometimes to reduce the "host" rock—if the phrase may be permitted about so uninvited an intrusion—into a kind of breccia or shatter-conglomerate. As usual in such cases, there is plenty of evidence that the acid magma has been affected by "digestion" of the basic material into which it has been intruded.

Lastly, it would seem, in this record of stupendous Eocene vulcanicity came a reversion to basic intrusions, when a large assemblage of dykes, sills and veins of basalt or dolerite were injected alike into the gabbro and granophyre masses.

[1] Reference may here be made to A. C. O'Dell and K. Walton, *The Highlands and Islands of Scotland*, (1962), pp. 319–25. St Kilda and its inhabitants, the remotest community in Great Britain, have always attracted attention; and the literature about the island group is extensive.

In spite of statements to the contrary, no sedimentary rocks have so far been recorded from these islands.

Strange though it may seem, it is possible that the St Kilda group of islands escaped the over-all Pleistocene glaciation, though undoubtedly it had its local ice-streams. A botanical survey of the islands has prompted the suggestion that their flora derives uninterruptedly from Pliocene times. Some of the plants, such as the lesser celandine, vetch and honeysuckle, have been thought to be survivals from a former woodland ground flora; but of course these may have been introduced by birds, or indeed, by human agency. Apparently no heather is found on the islands, which are clad in a bright green garb of grass, sedges and rushes.

But it is the fauna of St Kilda, and particularly its bird life, which is of supreme importance, and justifies the National Trust in the jealous care now being taken for its preservation. On Soay, their last native habitat in Britain, lived the half-wild mouflon sheep, a strange and primitive breed found in prehistoric settlements on the European mainland, and in the midden dumps or refuse pits of the Roman fort at Newstead near Melrose. Long-haired and fawn coloured, of small size but long-legged and goat-like in their movements, with large downward-curved and forward-pointing horns, these creatures were hunted with dogs, sometimes even with guns, by the St Kildans. At the evacuation in 1930, most of them were brought across from Soay to Hirta, where they are carefully preserved: the stock now may amount to over 1,300.

St Kilda boasts its own peculiar species of field-mouse, *Apodemus sylvaticus Hirtensis,* which is being carefully protected by the Nature Conservancy. It is described in the following terms:[1]

When mature the St Kilda field-mouse weighs twice as much as a mainland one, and it has a larger ear and hind foot and a tail as long as its body. The upper surface of its coat is a warm reddish brown, and in place of the whitish underside of the typical race the warm brown continues underneath; or is replaced usually by a beautiful orange buff.

Furthermore, St Kilda possessed its own special kind of house-mouse: but alas! since the evacuation of the islanders in 1930 this little animal must now be regarded as extinct. No doubt a mouse

[1]Williamson and Boyd, p. 135.

A Uist Landscape

is a humble and unregarded creature: yet once any animal, or any species of an animal, has become extinct, in the evolutionary process, it can never be replaced: and, to that extent, what Thomson finely called "the long review of ordered life" is forever abridged.

St Kilda possesses a unique species of wren, *Troglodytes hirtensis*. In the early years of the present century this charming little bird was almost extinguished by the ruthless raids of collectors, who shot the birds and plundered their eggs; until in 1904 a special Act of Parliament was passed protecting them from the shot gun and the nest harrier. Fortunately, this legal protection, and the vigilance of the Nature Conservancy, seem likely to protect the St Kilda wren for the future. A more unfortunate story is the fate of the Great Auk or Garefowl (*Pinguinus impennis*). This large handsome bird was unable to fly; it laid only a single egg; its flesh was succulent; it supplied oil for lamps; and its feathers were valuable. So in North America it was pursued with such recklessness that it became extinct there early in the nineteenth century. In Scotland its remains are frequent in prehistoric kitchen middens; but owing to its vulnerability it was already in decline by the seventeenth century. In the course of the next century this noble bird became less and less common in the Northern Isles and Hebrides; and the last individual known in Britain is said to have been caught on St Kilda in 1840. Now the Great Auk and its beautifully mottled egg are to be found only, and as a great rarity, in some of our leading museums.

The sea birds of St Kilda afforded the main source of food to the islanders: their skins and feathers even served in part to clothe them. Razor-bills and gannets, guillemots, solan geese, puffins and fulmars, here nest in amazing abundance. The St Kildans were consummate fowlers, prepared to take incredible risks in descending their dreadful cliffs to club or snare the birds and to collect their eggs. Out of gannet skins they made themselves shoes, and from their feathers socks. The fulmars provided them with oil for their lamps. With such an abundance of ready-to-hand food, the islanders kept no hens, and little fishing was practised—almost none from boats (which in this treeless land had to be imported), but a limited amount by angling from the rock ledges. Cattle and sheep were kept on the rich pasture land; but goats not, for these active climbing animals disturbed the birds. As in Shetland, the sheep were plucked, not sheared. Latterly

12

Castlebay, Barra

there were no horses, which were thought to damage the pasture. Only a few acres on the outskirts of the village were devoted to agriculture. The crops were bere or barley, oats, potatoes, cabbages and turnips, all manured by peat-ash and dung. Right up to the evacuation in 1930, the St Kildans ground their grain in rotary querns.

The only inhabited site in historic times was on Hirta, round the south-eastern or Village Bay. At first the dwellings were of the normal "black house" type. The thatch was sometimes secured with gannets' beaks! In 1863 the laird provided the community with neat zinc-roofed cottages: but the metal failed to stand up to the weather, and was soon replaced by tarred felt. As elsewhere in the Hebrides, many of the old "black houses" were retained as byres. A distinctive architectural feature of Hirta, a real note of interest in its vacant landscape, was provided by the "cleats". These were small, cylindrical or ovoid store houses, with high turf roofs. In the cleats the St Kildans kept their eggs, salted seafowl, meat, hay, corn and peats, and even their fishing nets and the precious driftwood. Built without mortar, these curious structures admitted the wind, while depriving it of its moisture, and so kept their contents dry. About 750 cleats, whole or in ruin, have been recorded, scattered over Hirta. A selection are now being preserved by the National Trust.

We have seen how the great eighteenth century poet of nature, James Thomson, himself a Scot, was interested in the Hebrides, and knew something about St Kilda. In his *Autumn* he has given a singularly accurate sketch of the islanders and their mode of subsistence, so largely dependent on birds:

> Or where the Northern Ocean, in vast whirls
> Boils round the naked melancholy isles
> Of farthest Thule, and the Atlantic surge
> Pours in among the stormy Hebrides,
> Who can recount what transmigrations there
> Are annual made? What nations come and go?
> And how the living clouds on clouds arise?
> Infinite wings! till all the plume-dark air,
> And rude-resounding shore, are one wild cry.
>   Here the plain harmless native, his small flock,
> And herd diminutive of many hues,
> Tends on the little island's verdant swell,
> The shepherd's sea-girt reign; or to the rocks

Dire-clinging, gathers his ovarious food,
Or sweeps the fishy shore; or treasures up
The plumage, rising full, to form the bed
Of Luxury.

Little is known about the early history of St Kilda. A survey of
its antiquities will be made in due course, it is hoped, by the Royal
Commission on the Ancient and Historical Monuments of Scotland. What seems to be an undoubted earthhouse of Iron Age
type has been excavated: and on Gleam Mor, or the northern side
of Hirta, Messrs Williamson and Morton Boyd have carefully
planned a group of multiple circular huts which look extremely
archaic, but whose absolute date is quite uncertain. These could
well represent an older village centre than the one abandoned in
1930. On Dun there is the remnant of a hill-fort. Three ancient
church sites are known, all on the outskirts of the village. They are
dedicated respectively to Christ, to St Brendan the Voyager and
to St Columba. The place names are part Celtic and part Norse.
From an unknown period St Kilda belonged to Macleod of
Dunvegan; but in 1934 it was sold to the fifth Marquis of Bute,
who on his death in 1956 bequeathed the islands to the National
Trust for Scotland, who in their turn, as stated above, leased them
to the Nature Conservancy. Also, as already stated, an area on
Hirta is now in the hands of the Ministry of Defence, and is used
in tracking guided missiles launched from Benbecula.

Of the social condition of the islanders ample information has
been preserved, from the sixteenth century onwards. In the main
they were a self-supporting community, providing their own
food, clothing, fuel and gear. Their exports were cattle, a certain
amount of salted fish (cod and ling), cheese, tallow, sea-bird oil,
wool, sheepskins, feathers, rough undyed tweed, cloth and knitwear. Rents were paid mostly in cloth and feathers, collected by
Macleod's factor on his annual visit. Imports were tobacco and
whisky, meal, tea, sugar and salt, paraffin, metal tools, hardware
and such simple household furniture as the islanders could not
make for themselves. On one occasion a benefactor provided the
St Kildans with a complete outfit of domestic crockery, including
chamber pots. Not having the least idea for what these latter
utensils could have been intended, the islanders ate their porridge
out of them!

Communication with the outside world was maintained by a boat sent twice yearly by the laird, and also by means of the frequent calls paid by trawlers. When General Campbell landed on Hirta in 1746, in the course of the man-hunt for Prince Charles Edward Stuart, he found the islanders unaware that a civil war had taken place. As late as 1909 the Old Style calendar continued in use, Hogmanay being celebrated on 12th January.

Sometimes messages were sent out in a hollow block of wood, attached to an inflated sheep's bladder. It is said that on one such occasion a letter reached its destination *via* Norway! Latterly, mail was carried to and fro from the island by trawlers from Aberdeen. After a disastrous famine in 1912 which drew nation-wide attention to St Kilda, and was followed by a severe outbreak of influenza, a wireless station was established on Hirta. This, however, attracted the attention of a German submarine on 18th May, 1918, during the First World War, and did not survive that cataclysm.

After the Disruption the Free Kirk, as elsewhere in the Hebrides, held the St Kildans in thrall. It is right, however, to say that some of its ministers were men of sterling and stalwart character, who served their flock with fidelity and devotion. So did the schoolmasters, and the, alas! too infrequent nurses. Left inevitably to themselves, the islanders managed their own affairs, meeting daily in what has been described as "the St Kildan Parliament". They had their own body of customary law, based largely upon the Mosaic code, and their economy was at once republican and socialistic. Serious crime was unknown among the little community; and many visitors have testified to their mutual helpfulness and their hospitality to strangers—particularly to those cast upon their iron shores by shipwreck. On one notable occasion, in 1887, nine Austrian sailors were thus maintained upon the island for nearly six weeks.

Up to the middle of the nineteenth century the St Kildans appear to have enjoyed a reasonable, if modest, standard of living. They are described as well nourished and well clothed, and this impression is confirmed by numerous extant photographs. In these, the men look stocky and stalwart. Many of the young women are comely—though, as elsewhere in the Hebrides, the gross overburden of physical toil imposed upon them by their lazy men-folk caused them soon to forfeit their good looks.

In the latter part of the nineteenth century a decline set in, due, as it would seem, to a complex of causes: to recurrent epidemics; to the endemic scourge of infantile tetanus, overcome only after prolonged resistance to treatment by the parents of the helpless sufferers,[1] in 1891; to successive failures of the harvest; and possibly to long-continued inbreeding. The spirit of the people began to fail. Their standard of cleanliness, never very high, grew worse. At the same time, owing to increasing contacts with the outer world, their material wants became greater than their insular resources could supply. Of money they had little: and its purchasing power was remorselessly eroded by that curse of modern times, creeping inflation. The population steadily dwindled. In the mid-nineteenth century it had numbered about 110; by 1921 the total was 71, and a decade later it had shrunk to under 50.

After the First World War it became clear that evacuation was the only solution to the intractable problem of St Kilda. With the consent of the thirty-six inhabitants, this operation, which aroused world-wide interest, was carried out on 29th August, 1930, at a cost to the Government of just under £1,000.[2] They were transported to Ardtornish in Morven, where, natives of a treeless island, they were set to work by the Forestry Commission. Their subsequent history on this new environment is one of pathos, if not indeed of tragedy. In the main, the population was an aging one: many died soon after the transportation; others drifted back, homesick, to their deserted homesteads in St Kilda, at least during the summer season. Of the younger men, seven served their country during the Second World War.

So now, except for the military personnel, the officials of the Nature Conservancy, and summer parties organized by the National Trust, St Kilda is a scene of utter loneliness and piteous ruins—ruins all the more pathetic because they are not like the bare windswept skeleton of some ancient castle, or the sand-blown remains of a prehistoric settlement such as Skara Brae, the life once lived in which is utterly remote from our present thoughts. They are the ruined homesteads, barns and byres, the factor's house, the church and manse, school and schoolhouse, of

[1] "If it is God's will that babies should die, nothing that you can do will save them", the nurse was told.

[2] The story has been told, with sympathy and eloquence, by Alasdair Alpin Macgregor, the special correspondent of *The Times*, in his moving book, *A Last Voyage to St. Kilda, 1931*.

a community of our own time, whose mode of existence, whose portraits are familiar to us, and the tale of whose slow decay and final extinction has caught our imagination and wrung our heart-strings. It is satisfactory that the National Trust is doing all in its power to preserve these pathetic memorials of a vanished race.

The Strange Case of Lady Grange

Much the most famous episode in the meagre history of St Kilda is the detention there, for seven long years, of the unfortunate Lady Grange. Many legends have gathered round this extraordinary happening, but it has recently been carefully investigated by Dr I. M. Grant in her splendid history of the Macleods. Lady Grange was Rachel, a daughter of Christy of Dalry, and had married a distinguished lawyer, a Senator of the College of Justice, Lord Grange. He was a younger brother of "Bobbing Jock", the luckless Earl of Mar of the "Fifteen", and was himself suspected of Jacobite sympathies. His wife, though in her younger days a beauty and a wit, was a lady of unbalanced mind, given to drink and violent in temper, and their marriage proved an unhappy one. In the course of a quarrel she threatened to reveal some of her husband's clandestine dealings with the Jacobites. So in 1732 he had her forcibly abducted and carried, first to Castle Tioram in Moidart (see *supra*, p. 34), thence to Heisker off North Uist, and finally, after two years of captivity there, to St Kilda, where, with the connivance of Macleod of Dunvegan, she was detained, in miserable loneliness among a people of whose language she was ignorant, until 1742. She was supplied with food and given a two-roomed hut and a female servant. In a letter alleged to have been written by her from St Kilda, she describes the place as "a viled, neasty, stinking poor isle". At last her lawyer in Edinburgh discovered her whereabouts, upon which she was hurriedly removed by her captors to Harris, and thence to Skye. Here she became quite insane. Receipts preserved at Dunvegan show that she was reasonably provided for. She was allowed a certain wandering freedom, but in 1745, thirteen years after her abduction, she died, and (as stated above, p. 62) was buried in Trumpan churchyard.

INDEX OF PLACES

INDEX OF PLACES